MASK
Making

MASK
Making

Glynn McKay

CHARTWELL
BOOKS, INC.

Published by
Chartwell Books, Inc.
A Division of Book Sales, Inc.
Raritan Center
114 Northfield Avenue
Edison, NJ 08818
USA

ISBN 0-7858-0176-6

Printed in Italy

Right
The author with some of the many
masks he has made.

Acknowledgements

Photographs on pages 6-8 are by courtesy of
The Bridgeman Art Library. Other photographs by
Michael Plomer, Richard Jackson and the author.

In listing materials needed for making projects
in this book quantities have not been specified
because they are so dependant upon the work
being undertaken. Read instructions fully before
obtaining materials and make your own
decisions. Do not hesitate to ask the advice of
suppliers.

The publishers have made every effort to insure
that all instructions given in this book are
accurate and safe, but they cannot accept
liability for any resulting injury, damage or loss
to either person or property whether direct or
consequential and howsoever arising. Materials
manufacturers' instructions should always be
carefully followed.

CONTENTS

MASKS AND MASK MAKING

The mask to hide or change the face is found in many cultures around the world. One African tradition tells how the first mask was painted on the bottom of a gourd water container to frighten and discipline a naughty child, others that masks were invented by members of a secret society to hide the identity of members when they inflicted punishments.

Masks have often had a religious and ritual significance, worn by shamans and participants in ceremonies representing ancestors and spirits who were thought to lose their own identity and take on that of the mask. Sometimes they have been thought to be charged with prophylactic properties, such as those once worn by Chinese children as protection from measles or the ferocious fanged masks of Sri Lanka, also worn against disease, while in Europe in the seventeenth century doctors sometimes worn a strange

A Roman mosaic of a group of actors rehearsing a satyr play. One wears a face mask pushed up on the head and there are masks for classical tragedy on the table and on the floor.

beaked mask as a supposed protection at times of plague.

Funerary masks were laid over the faces of the mummified dead of ancient Egyptian, of buried Mycenean Greek rulers and of Inca royalty in Peru.

Theatre had its origins in religious ritual and the drama of ancient Greece was performed by masked actors, the stylized features indicated to the audience what the character was and enabling one actor to play several roles within the drama. The ancient No theatre of Japan uses very simple masks, the dance drama of Bali very elaborate ones. Devils and demons in the mystery plays of the middle ages wore masks – and often other characters too, while the Italian theatre of the *commedia dell' arte* developed a range of character masks which partially covered the face.

The No retains a religious element: the stage is consecrated before each performance and the all-male actors meditate before their masks before putting them on. Even in the modern western theatre actors using masks find that concentrating

carefully on the mask helps them to take on the character of the mask and, like the tribal dancer, becoming, as it were, inhabited by its spirit.

Wearing a mask alters the nature of acting. A simple mask can add concentration to a performance for the actor must move differently and, though the mask enlarges the effect of other elements of gesture and performance, the mask itself, rather than appearing blank, can seem to alter with quite small changes of head position and accompanying body language.

The wearing of masks at carnivals such as Mardi Gras again has roots in religious festivals. Disguised, participants have licence for behaviour not acceptable in their own persona, while at Halloween the frightening can be made powerless by confronting it with its own mask. But the social wearing of the mask at carnival and at

A carved and painted wooden mask used in dance ceremonies by the Zombo people in Africa.

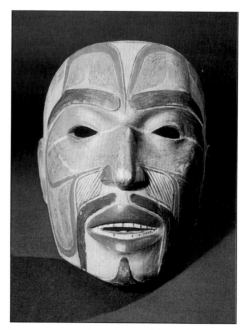

A wooden portrait mask carved by the Kwakuiti Native Americans of British Columbia 1825-75. The painted patterns immediately indentified the person it depicted.

6

masked balls had more to do with the freedom of behaviour that was given because the identity of the wearer was concealed.

Even the simplest of masks, just covering the eyes, can make identification difficult, and the half mask, adapted from that of the *commedia dell' arte,* frequently seen at the Venetian carnival, gave even more concealment. It, together with the cloak with which it was so often worn gained the name domino.

In the renaissance courts of Europe a mask mounted on a central stick or side stick and held before the face was often carried at masked balls, allowing the wearer to conceal or reveal their identify with ease.

Masks can represent anything, from a blank emptiness to the most elaborate representation of human, animal, monster or abstract concept. They have been made of all kinds of materials. Those found in the royal tombs at Mycenae were of beaten gold. In Chinese Imperial tombs jade masks were found. Native American and many Polynesian and African masks were carved from wood, as were those of the No theatre. No one is sure what Greek theatrical masks were made from but the Pulchinellos and Arlecchinos of the Italian *commedia* wore masks of moulded leather. Cloth, leaves, paper, feathers, shells and metals all appear in tribal masks but in recent times, until the development of mouldable rubbers and plastics, theatrical and carnival masks have tended to be made of cloth or paper, large heads for carnival parades, and animal characters for the theatre often being made of *papier mâche'*. Now rubber latex, fibreglass and plastics are increasingly used in making moulded masks which can reproduce considerable detail and be made in multiples if needed.

In designing and making a mask the first consideration is its purpose. How that affects design will be particular to the circumstances of its use, its theatrical or social role, whether it is to represent, enhance, mystify or disguise. Its appearance

will be related to role, setting, overall costume and creative concept but some considerations apply to all masks.

First, what is to be done while wearing the mask? If it is to be worn for a short time by someone who does not need to move or speak in it, it does not greatly matter if the wearer's sight is hampered and if the mask is not ventilated. However, if worn by someone who has to undertake energetic physical action the airways

must be free and they may need to see easily to move about.

It may be possible to make large holes over the whole eye socket, or even wider, and use make-up on the face to match the mask. Sometimes it may be necessary, as in some animal masks for instance, to place sight holes not in the eyes but elsewhere in the mask. In a mask that stands away from the face and when used in bright light, it may be possible to use a gauze section over part of the mask which

Puchinella in Love by Giovanni Tiepolo (1727-1804)
The characters of the **Commedia dell' arte** wear the traditional leather half-masks of this improvised theatre form.

A Masked Ball in St Mark's Square by V. Ponga,
painted in the nineteenth century for the Caffe Quadri in Venice. Masks worn by the revellers ran range from a simple cover across the eyes to near full face masks, with many like those of the **Commedia.** The white masks, worn with the black hat and cape were the way in which Venetians hid their identity.

will appear solid when viewed from a short distance away but which will allow the wearer to see outwards.

If the wearer is to sing or speak then a mask which stops above the mouth or is cut out around it may be necessary, or even one which sits over the nose but leaves the nostrils clear. Sometimes, especially for small children or in the presentation of very small animals, the design solution may be to push the whole mask up onto the forehead and head with no attempt to hide the face below.

The choice of material in which to make a mask will be determined by the ability of the medium to carry the detail and form required of the design, the degree of comfort it affords and the strength and durability demanded, whether for a single social evening or for a theatrical run of months or even years.

The very simplest mask to make is a rectangle or a figure-of-eight with eye-holes cut in it and ties or an elastic attached to the sides to keep it on the head. These can be varied in shape and decorated to become very elaborate pieces despite the simplicity of their basic form. Almost as simple is the half-or full-face paper mask, like those so often made for children, curved over the face or if more stylized bent down the nose line, with eye-slits or holes and sufficient airspace to permit easy breathing. A plain white triangle with token features indicated can be surprisingly effective. Such masks need no skill or special knowledge in making.

The next stage in mask-making is to mould the mask to fit the face. This book begins with a simple half mask, made on the face of the wearer, though a similar form could be made over a face cast. It uses plaster bandages but the same form could be

Simple masks by the author
Top: An elfin mask which although it covers the nose, leaves the nostrils clear.
Centre: A latex mask covering the full face and enabling an instant change of character for the wearer.
Top: A three quarter mask for a play on a Frankenstein like theme.

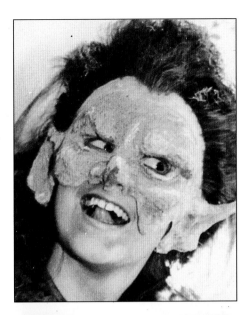

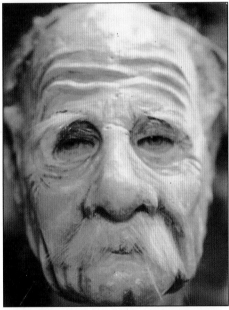

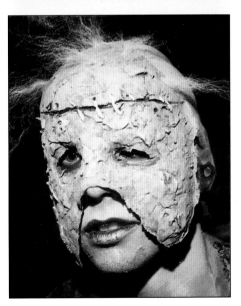

made off the face with paper and glue or papier mâche'.

The following chapters then describe the making of a life mask, ways of building up a paper mask on a sculpted base, the casting of moulds to make both face and full-head masks, and the moulding of them in a variety of materials. These masks can be kept on the head by bands around the head or by attachment to a headpiece, the making of which is also described, or in the case of whole-head masks will be supported entirely on the head.

All the face masks, except for those moulded in soft rubber, could be mounted on a central or side stick and carried in the hand in front of the face.

The modelling of mask forms in wet clay or in Plasticine is much easier than most people think. Painting and drawing require skill in translating three dimensional forms into a two dimensional representation but in modelling and sculpting in these pliable materials you can adapt and adjust all the time, changing your mind and correct errors until you are happy with the result (unlike the wood-carved forms used for Italian leather masks which require great carving skills). If not experienced, you will probably find it easier to work with your fingers but modelling tools will be helpful to achieve particular effects.

Some of the materials used in making these masks can be dangerous and should NOT be used by children. Everyone should observe the safety instructions given, ensure that workplaces are always well ventilated and take care that flammable materials are not left about.

Though materials may be obtainable through theatrical suppliers many are sold in other stores and a list of sources from which they can be obtained is given at the end of the book.

A SIMPLE MASK MADE ON A FACE

Slightly more sophisticated than the simple `Lone Ranger' type of mask of card or cloth and the flat mask cut out of card is one which is moulded to fit the face. The most convenient way of making one is to have a three-dimensional sculpture of a face on which to model. The ideal, for a perfect fit, is to work with a cast of the actual face which will wear the mask.

The making of a face cast is described on page 18, but if a single mask is all that is required and you or the potential wearer do not wish to go to the trouble of making a face cast, you can mould a mask directly on the face. The first method to be described is especially suitable for a half-mask when the nostrils and mouth are not covered by the mask, but will not be as durable as the methods described later using latex and Celastic.

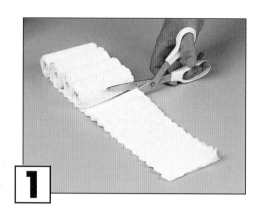

Explain to him or her exactly what you are going to do. There is nothing dangerous about it if you take proper care but it can be disconcerting to have a mask made on you, so knowing what is happening will be reassuring and prevent your subject panicking.

From a roll of plaster bandage cut lengths of about 12 in (30cm) long that will go over the front of the face and around the top of the head. It is quicker to unroll several rolls laying them on top of each other or folding bandage back on itself to cut four lengths at once. [1] You will need 12-16 lengths, but it does not matter if you cut more, you can always use them on another occasion (provided that they are kept in an airtight box to prevent them getting damp.)

Wrap clingfilm (Saran Wrap) over the head of your subject and down over the eyes as far as you intend the mask to go. [2] You may take film to the tip of the nose and lower on either side but do not carry it down over the nostrils.

When you are experienced and have become faster in making this kind of mask, it may be possible to make a mask coming lower on the face – but you must keep the cling film and bandage clear of the nostrils, even if your subject breathes through the mouth to make a fuller mask – but no-one should attempt that to begin with!

MATERIALS NEEDED

Clingfilm (Saran Wrap)

Old sheet, towel – or a plastic garbage bag to protect clothes

Plaster bandage

Bowl of water

Scissors

Craft knife

Paints and other materials for decoration

Preparation

Set out your materials on a clear worktop and settle the person on whom you are making the mask comfortably on a chair. Wrap him or her in a cloth or cut a head hole in a plastic garbage sack and pull it over the head and then tuck a towel around the neck. If he or she wears contact lenses they must be taken out and of course any ordinary glasses should be removed.

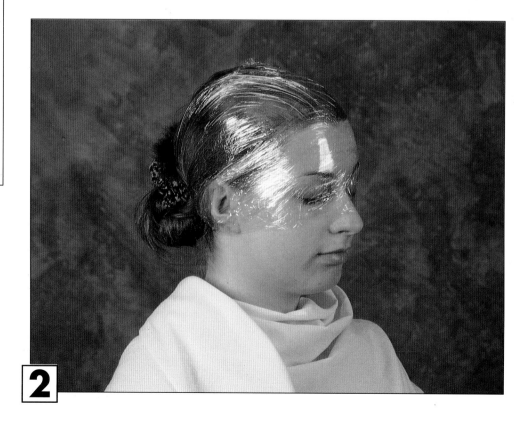

3

Making the mask

Take four strips of plaster bandage, lay them on top of each other and, keeping the ends between your thumbs and forefingers, dip them into the bowl of water and then squeeze them out.[3] Place them, as one, over the top of the head and smooth them down. Now wet, squeeze and apply another block of four below the first and very slightly overlapping it [4] – and so on down the face, gently pressing to mould their shape over the eyes and nose, until you have covered the face as far as you want to mask to extend.

If you prefer you could lay them singly, butting successive rows and placing the next layer over the joins. This makes a slightly smoother finish but takes much longer. Either way, build up a thickness of four layers.

WARNING
Do NOT put plaster bandages under the jawline or more than half way around the head or you will not be able to remove the finished mask.

Tell your subject when have completed applying the bandages and explain that they must be allowed to dry, which should only take two or three minutes. With a soft pencil or felt-tip pen mark the outline of the eye sockets as a guide to where the eye holes should be cut.[5]

When the bandages have hardened ask the wearer to hold the mask gently onto his or her face and with the round-ended blade of a pair of scissors tucked beneath the bottom edge of the clingfilm (Saran Wrap) cut

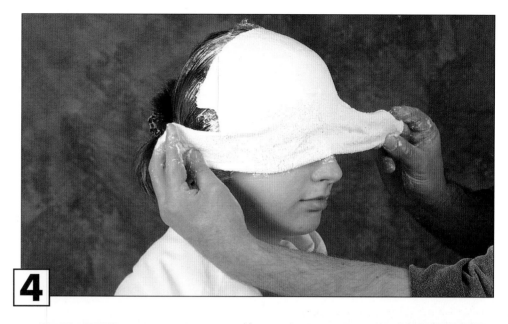

4

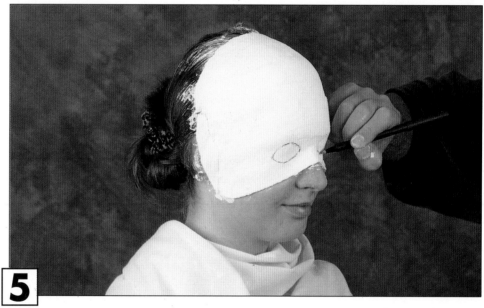

5

it apart from the rear – take care not to cut the subject's hair! The mask can then fall forward into the hands holding it. You will have made a mask which covers the front of the head and forehead and the upper part of the face.

When it is completely dry cut out. eyeholes [6] with a craft knife and trim the outer edges to the shape you require. Attach a string, ribbon or a band of velcro on either side with a glue gun or a stapler. These tie or grip behind the head to keep it firmly in place. If you use staples then glue a piece of chamois leather or similar soft fabric, or a piece of sticking

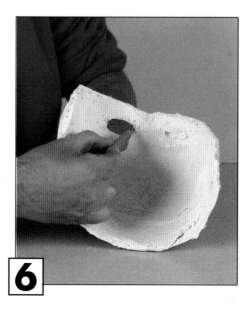

6

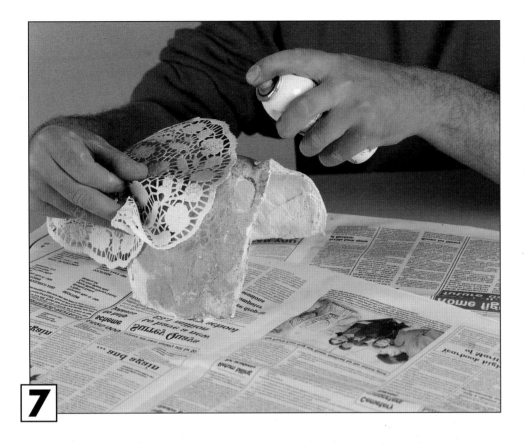

plaster, over the inner wires so that they cannot scratch. Painting the whole of the inside of the mask with a rubber adhesive, such as copydex, and applying cut pieces of chamois leather fitted together like a jigsaw will make the mask both stronger and more comfortable in wear. Fitting small pieces together is easier than trying to make a single piece fit into all the contours, which is difficult to do without creating creases and ridges.

Now you can paint or decorate the mask in any way you like. You may want a realistic representation – human or animal, but plain, patterned and abstract masks can all be very effective.

The head part could be decorated to form a headdress or a headdress could be worn partly covering it.

The mask shown here was painted with spray-on hair colourant and then a paper doilly used as a stencil through which to spray a second colour.[7]

7

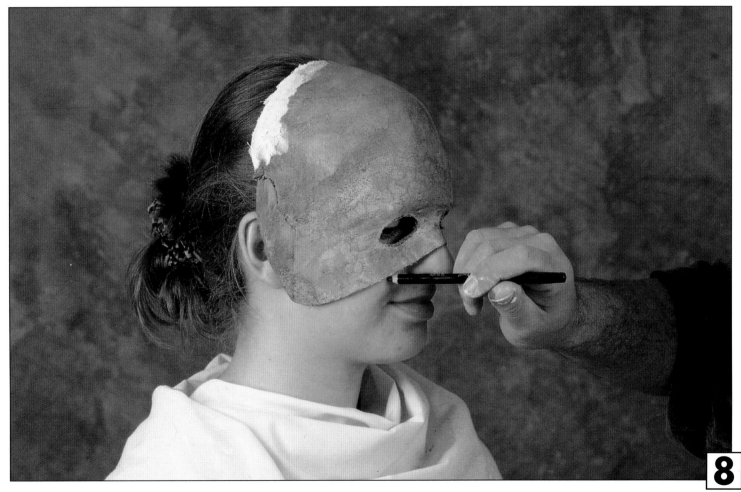

8

The method described here can, of course, be used for making masks covering as little of the face as you require. Even a simple domino will gain from being modelled to the wearer's contours.

Decorating the face below the mask.

A half-mask can be worn on its own, or the rest of the face can be made up to match it or complement it. If you want an effect that differs from conventional make-up or face paint you can quite safely apply a `make-up' of coloured tissue paper.

Place the completed half mask on the subject's head and mark the position of the edge of the mask onto the face with an eyebrow pencil, as a guide to how much of the face must be made-up.[8]

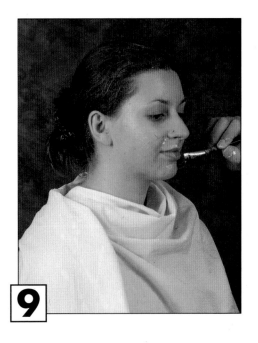

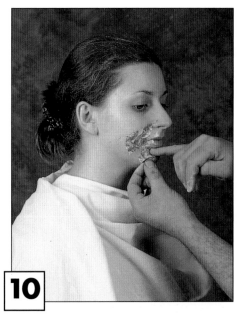

MATERIALS NEEDED
Clear honey or Spirit gum and remover (rubber surgical adhesive is ideal but expensive)
Art brush
Coloured tissue paper
Scissors

If the clothes to be worn with the mask have to be pulled over the head cover take care that they do not rub against the face as they are put on. Put on the mask and then, if you do not want the mask to be obviously a mask hide the edges with hair, or a headdress.

Removing the adhesive
If honey has been used it will simply wash off. If spirit gum has been used you will need to use the appropriate solvent, then wash thoroughly with soap and water. If the skin feels dry after you have removed the adhesive apply a moisturiser.

Spread honey or spirit gum over the lower part of the face which you wish to decorate, [9] but keep it away from the eyes. [10] Now tear the tissue paper into small pieces and press it against the honey or the surgical adhesive. [11] If you use patterned paper chose a design which will effectively blend with itself when torn.

You do not have to limit yourself to tissue paper. Fabrics, feathers, leaves and any light materials could be incorporated, especially if you are using proper adhesive instead of honey.

In the example photographed a spotted line marked in mascara [12 overleaf] separates the pattern from the mask but you should make your own design and may not wish to mark the transition.

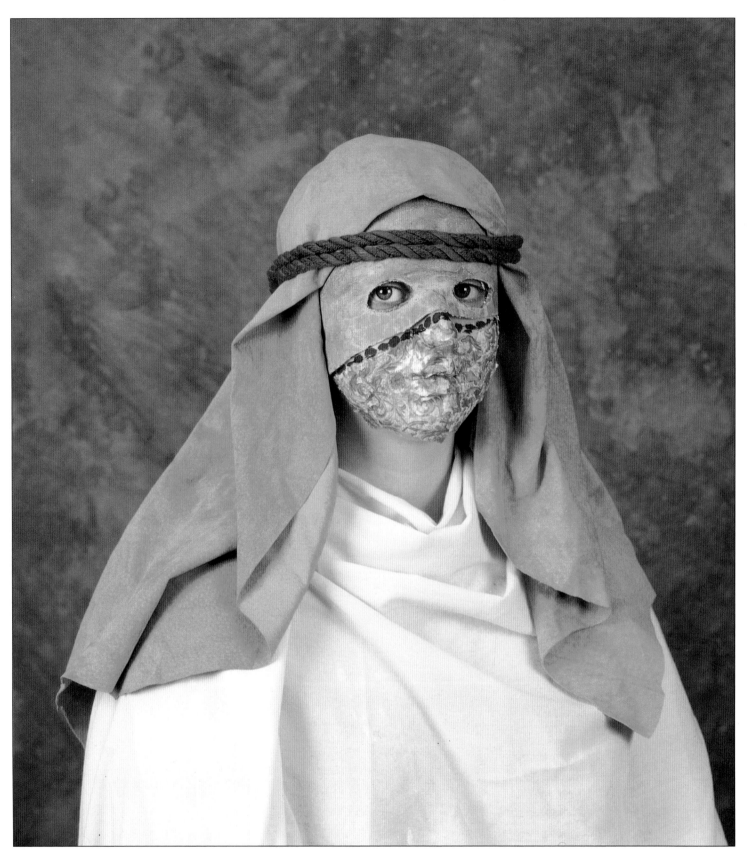

A half-made mask, on the face as described in the preceeding pages, the lower part of the face decorated with tissue paper.

A COMPLETE MASK MADE ON THE FACE

This uses the same principle as the preceding lower face `make-up' but requires more care and greater patience on the part of the wearer. When well made it can be removed in one piece and re-used, although it will not be very durable.

The technique is especially suitable for rapidly producing wrinkled skin and `horror' masks.

Preparation

Think out the way in which you want to decorate the face and decide on the materials you want to use. It may help to make a sketch beforehand but provided you have an idea in your mind of the effect you want you can improvise the actual creation as you go along.

Lay out materials and prepare your subject, making him or her comfortable. Cover the hair, preferably with a swim cap [1], or with clingfilm (Saran Wrap) if one is not available. Do NOT bring wrap down over the face.

Creating the mask

Tear up pieces of paper kitchen towel or cut pieces of muslin. Spread honey over the wearer's face and the cap to act as an adhesive. [1]

MATERIALS NEEDED

Swim cap
Clingfilm (Saran Wrap)
Kitchen roll, Muslin
Honey,
Latex or rubber adhesive (Copydex)
Cotton wool pads
Talcum powder
Acrylic paint
Coloured hair spray
Mascara,
String, wool or hair

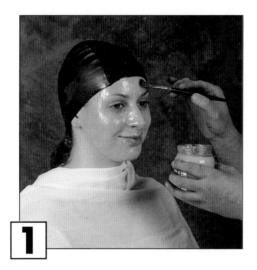

1

Place cotton wool pads over the eyes. The honey will keep them in place. [2]

Now press pieces of paper towel, tissue paper or muslin onto the honey all over the face and as much of the cap or filmwrap as you wish. You can cover the eyebrows but leave the eyelids and immediately around the eyes clear. If you want to make a smooth stylized mask then smooth the paper as you apply it but for a hundred-year old wrinkled face or a `horror' look let the paper crease and form ridges like aged skin, scars and deformities. [3]

Now paint rubber latex or Copydex over the layer of paper to seal it. If you want a wrinkled effect let the latex add to it, but take great care not to get any in the eyes which should still be covered by cotton wool pads. [4]

If you wish, you can alter the contour of the face or increase distortion, adding thickness where you require it by building up layers of paper and latex. As you proceed you can speed the drying of the latex with a hair-dryer.

When you have finished applying latex, powder over the mask with talcum to take away any stickiness. Remove the eye pads and you can

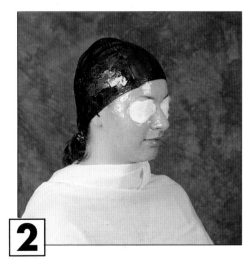

2

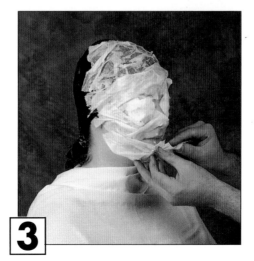

3

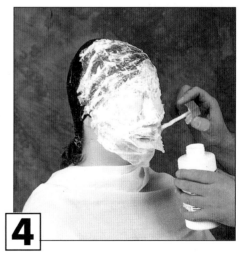

4

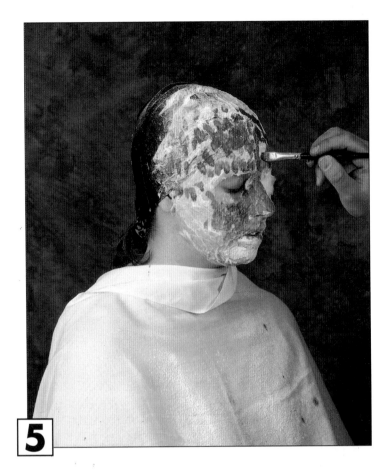

5

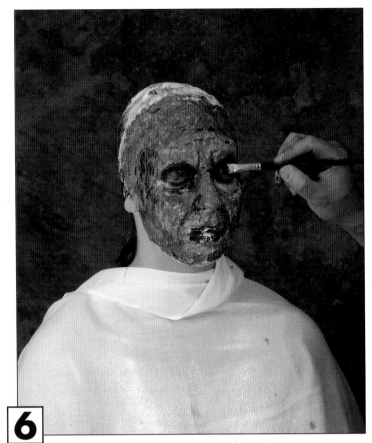

6

9

then add colouring. Since you are working on the surface of the mask, not on the skin, you do not have to use make-up or face paints but can use any water-based paints. [5] Around the eye, where you are working on the skin itself, make up or face paints must be used. [6]

To complete the look and hide the edges, instead of a headdress you can add locks of `hair' or string or fabric, glued over the swim cap with Copydex. [7]. When gluing `hair' to the eyebrows hold a cotton wool pad over the eye to protect it from any drips. [8]. Hold the hank of hair over the eyebrow and lightly press on the ends, placed at the appropriate angle, to ensure contact with the adhesive. Trim with scissors.

When the mask is removed wipe off the honey and wash thoroughly with soap and water. Use a moisturiser afterwards if the skin feels dry.

If a mask made in this way is removed very carefully removed and powdered inside to counter the

16

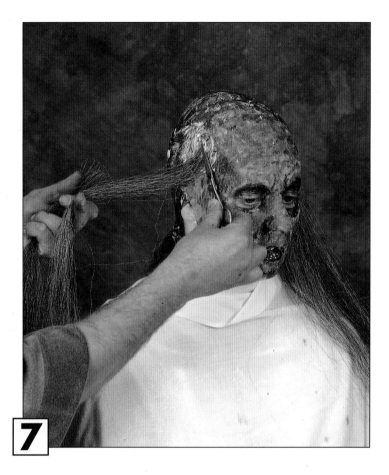

7

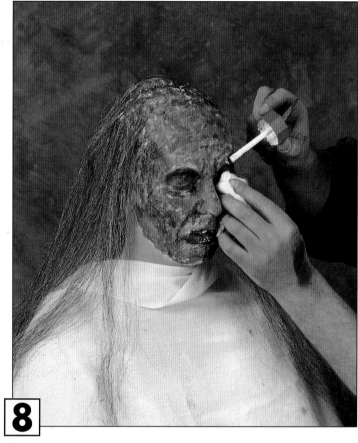

8

stickiness of the honey, it could possibly be used again.

WARNING
Some people, usually of fair complexion, are allergic to rubber latex which may make their skin go red. If this happens do not try to use this way of mask making again on that subject but make masks by one of the alternative methods.

> The use of paper and latex to built up wrinkles and textures can also be applied on masks made by the other methods described later in this book.

A 'horror' mask made using the technique employing wrinkled paper and rubber-based adhesive described for the proceeding mask made on the face, but applied on a Celastic mask.

FACE CASTING THE EASY WAY

To ensure a comfortable fit for any mask which is to be worn on the face it is necessary to make it to match the contours of the wearer and to match the size and positions of the eyes and mouth. The object here is to make a cast of the subject's face on which future masks can be modelled. This involves applying material directly to the face to create a mould from life and then to take a cast from that mould.

Adults have bigger faces than children and women differ from men but it will not usually be necessary to use an exact face cast and if you have already made several on different people you may be able to match a face of similar type rather than cast anew.

For most people having a cast made of the face is a disconcerting and rather tedious process. He or she must keep the face still throughout the operation with the eyes shut. The traditional way of keeping an airway open to enable her or him to breath while the face was covered was to insert straws in the nostrils but with care this is unnecessary. It was easy to knock the straws out and often more of a discomfort than a help. However, it is important to ensure that your subject is comfortable.

MATERIALS NEEDED

Clingfilm (Saran Wrap) or other covering for the hair
Dental alginate (slow-setting)
Plaster of Paris (or dental plaster for a stronger cast)
Plaster bandages
Petroleum jelly (Vaseline)
Shellac or Polyurethane varnish
Cold water
Tepid water (the temperature determines setting times of both the modelling and the casting materials, the warmer the water the faster it will be - beginners are advised to start by using fairly cold water)
Soap or washing-up liquid
3 flexible bowls
Another box or bowl to hold the finished mould (or use the alginate bowl again)
Large jug
Plaster knife or pocket knife
Rasp
Scissors
Brushes for applying plaster and shellac
Wooden modelling tool
Paper towel to clean up subject – and the person whose face is to be cast

Preparation

Get ready a clear working surface. A clean, dry Formica-topped table is ideal but any table protected by a sheet of polythene will do.

Take two plaster bandages and unroll one flat on the table. Place the other roll on top of it against the first and unroll to give a double thickness. Fold the ends back for about 12 in (30 cm) to give you four layers and cut the folds to give you 12in (30cm) lengths. Repeat this five times to give you 20 lengths in blocks of four, then cut one four layer length of 24 in (60cm). [1]

Set out your bowls and other tools and materials. In the first place 2-3 good handfuls of alginate. [2] One third fill the second bowl with cold water (for the plaster). The plaster mix is about one water to two plaster by volume. You will have to guess how much you need to fill the mould but make sure you have a large bowl for if it is more than two-thirds full you will slop plaster out of it. Half fill the last bowl with tepid water (with which to wet the plaster bandages).

Now you are ready for the person whose face you are going to cast. If your subject wears contact lenses ask him or her to remove them, and, of course, to take off any ordinary spectacles or face jewellery. Make

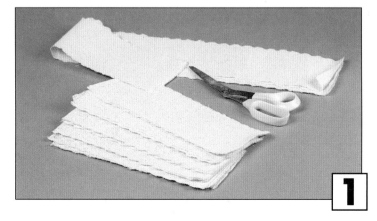

sure that they are not thirsty or likely to need the bathroom. Taking a mould will not take very long but it will seem much longer to the subject so it is essential to get them relaxed and seated really comfortably.

Use a cloth, a hairdresser's gown or a plastic garbage sack over their clothes to protect them from any splashes. If they have long hair pull it back and gather it behind in a chinon or into a ponytail held by an elastic band. While you are doing so explain carefully what is going to be involved and throughout the cast-making always say what you are doing.

Now you must protect your subject's hair. Use the clingfilm (Saran Wrap). Wrap it around the head just in front of the hairline and taking it over the ears, covering any sideburns if possible. Pulled tight [3], the film will cling to itself. You could use other materials for the job but this is cheaper and very easy to put on.

Apply a smear of Vaseline or other petroleum jelly to the eyebrows [4], eyelashes, hair exposed at the

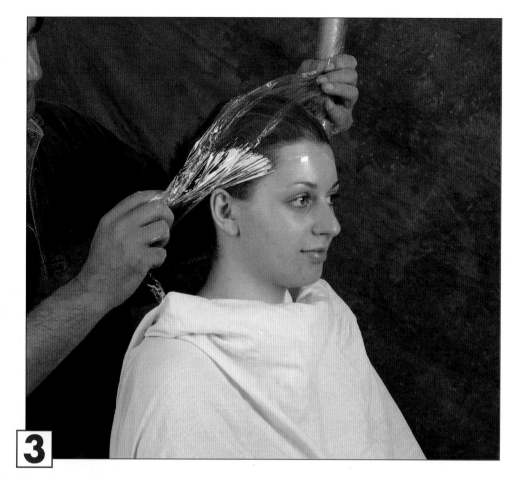

3

temples, sideburns, moustache, beard and any other facial hair under the chin. This will stop alginate from sticking to the hairs later. Do not overdo the petroleum jelly or the alginate will not make contact and will slide off the face. Wipe any excess jelly over the back of your own hands and wrists where plaster could also adhere as you mix and apply it.

Applying the alginate

Take the bowl with the dental alginate and gradually pour in cold water from the jug [5], mixing with the other hand as you do so, until you

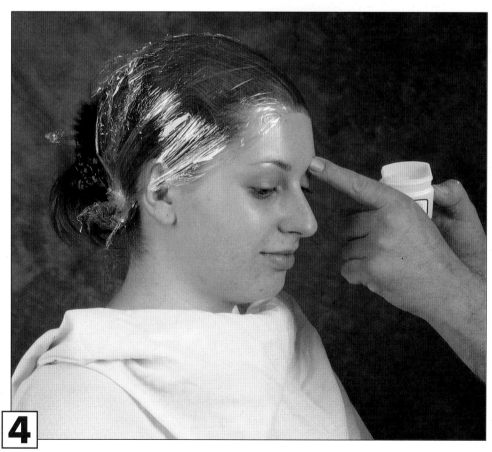

4

5

19

have a thick batter. [6] Add the water in a continuous stream and beat hard. It is difficult to add more water once mixed. You have only two to three minutes before the alginate sets so you need to work quickly – but be calm, don't rush!

When you have the right consistency start applying the mixture to the face.

Ask your subject to close his or her eyes and to keep them closed. The mouth must be kept closed too until after you have spread alginate over it, when the lips can be opened a little if this makes it easier to breathe.

Begin at the top of the forehead and work outwards and down. [7] Keep your touch gentle but firm. Let your finger tips feel the skin as in a massage – this will help to avoid any air pockets developing.

Pay particular attention to the eye sockets and ensure that you make a broad sweep outwards under the bottom lid, under the lash line, and nto the gap by the nose. Extend this sweep up over the eyebrows. As you

6

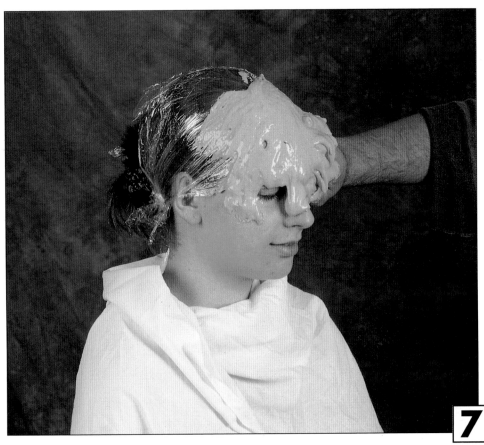

7

come down to the wings of the nose be careful not to completely obstruct the nostrils.

While applying the alginate keep an eye on the areas already covered. There will be a tendency for the material to flow downwards so smooth upwards to prevent it all ending around the neck! [8] If your subject is keeping their mouth open take care not to force alginate into it.

You will find this process much less complicated than it sounds and it will only take a couple of minutes once you have got used to it.

Applying the plaster bandages

While the alginate finishes setting cut a narrow strip of plaster bandage about 2 in (5cm) long and $^1/_3$ in (1 cm) wide and a couple of other 1 inch- (2.5 cm-) sided triangles. Now, with the alginate set, take the bandages you have prepared in groups of four and, keeping a grip of the ends in your fingers, immerse each set in turn in the bowl of tepid water. On immersion

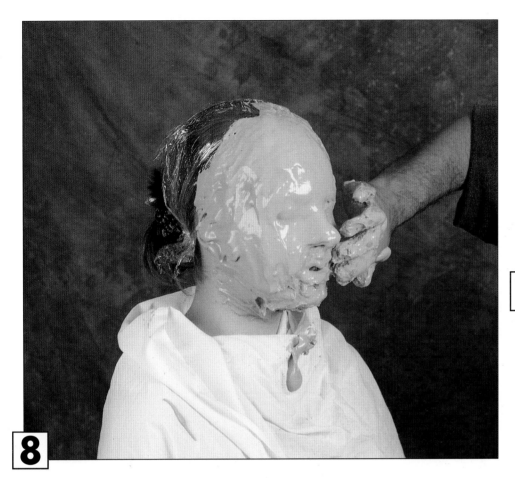

8

9

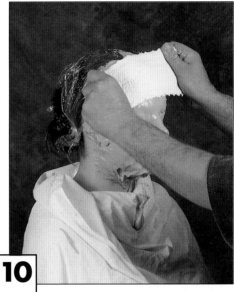

10

you will see a number of bubbles rising from the bandages. After they stop withdraw the bandage, still holding the ends, and wring out most, but not all, of the water. [**9**] Straighten the bandages out and apply them to the face in bands.

Start by placing bandages over the forehead. [**10**] Smooth them to the shape of the head using a circular rubbing with the finger tips. Overlap the next layer by about half an inch (15mm) and continue over the whole face, wetting more bandages as you need them. Mould them into the eye sockets, using the same circling finger motion. [**11**]

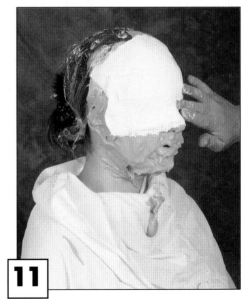

11

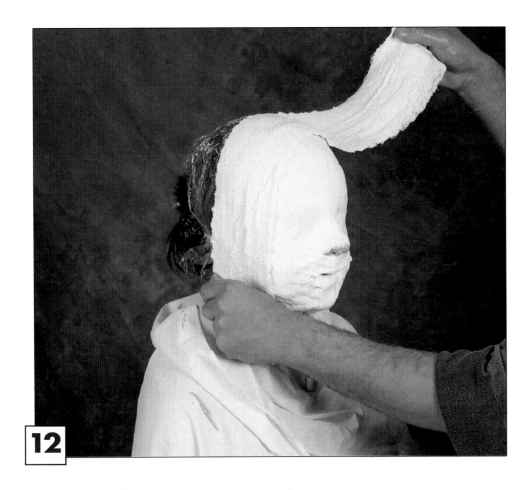

12

Pay particular attention to the nose and the area around it, finishing off with the small triangles you have just cut around the nostrils. Take care to keep the airways free. Use the longer 24in (60cm) strips to form an outer band around the edge of the cast. [12] The bandages will dry in place forming a support for the alginate beneath.

Finally, when the bulk of the bandages are set, lay the last thin strip of bandage over the centre of the nose between the nostrils and over the top lip. [13] This can be the most disconcerting of all for your subject, so keep it until the last moment just before you deem it time to remove the cast.

Removing your cast

To your subject's relief you can now ask him or her to hold the cast in both hands and to bend forward and `pull faces'. [14] This will help to detach the mask from the face and, with a little help, it will fall away. Your job is to loosen the edges and ease out any hair that may be stuck in the alginate – it should tease out quite easily. As the cast comes away try to keep the alginate in the `mother case' of bandages so that it does not tear.

Once it is free [15], lay the cast carefully aside and give your

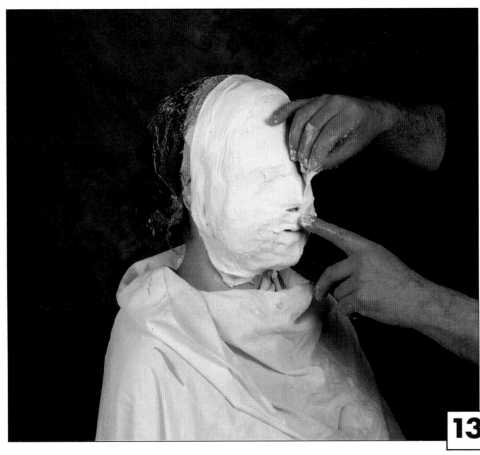

13

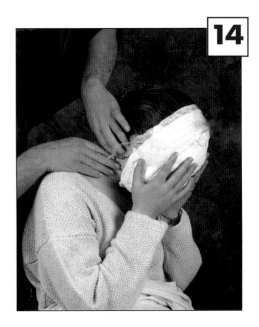

14

15

attention to your subject, helping to clean off any adhering alginate, removing Vaseline, the clingfilm and restoring things to normal.

Go on to make the cast as soon as possible. Alginate shrinks as it dries and if you leave it too long the cast will not match the subject but be of a smaller size.

Making the positive cast

What you have made is a negative of the contours of the face and you will now use that as a mould for casting a positive face.

First you need to fill the nostrils and the mouth (if your subject kept it

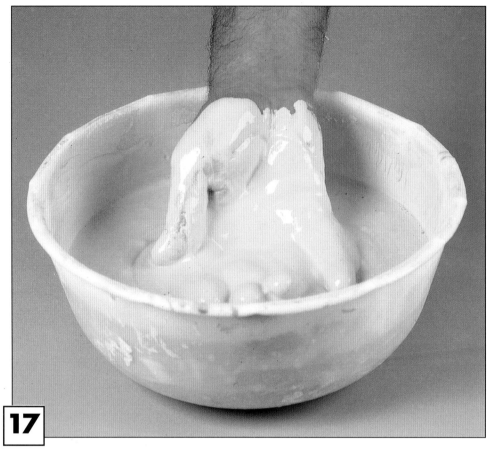

open) so that plaster does not run out of the holes. You can use a small piece of plaster bandage (or use some wet modelling clay if you have it). If you use bandage, let it dry before you use the mould. Place a towel or some cloth in another bowl or a box on which to support the mould and then you can mix your plaster.

Into the bowl you have not yet used, which should be already one third full of cold water, slowly add plaster of Paris, sifting it through your fingers into the water. [16] As it settles to the bottom, a large island of dry plaster will gradually form.

When you feel that the water is almost all absorbed dip your hand under the mixture and gently squeeze

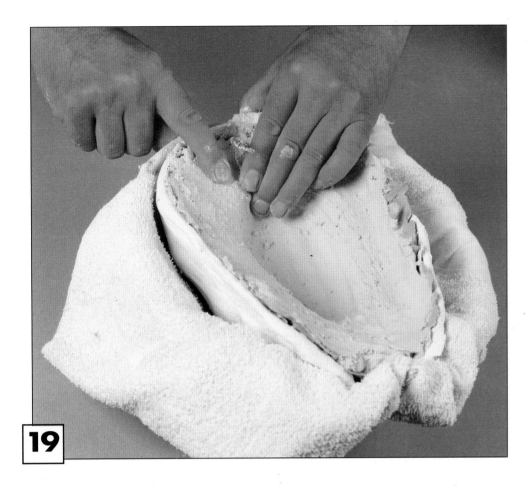

19

it through your fingers until it is smooth and creamy, which will also eliminate most of the air bubbles in it). [17] It is not easy to judge the precise moment to do this – that is one of those things that comes with experience.

After leaving the mixture to rest for a couple of minutes, sharply knock the bottom of the bowl against the floor. Do it several times. This will dislodge the last stubborn bubbles and leave your plaster ready for use.

Settle the mould into the padded bowl or box and begin to brush in the plaster with a soft brush so that you fill all the details of the mould [18], then slowly pour in the rest of the plaster to fill it. As it begins to harden you have the choice of pushing in a wire or string by which to hang up the finished cast [19], or of scooping out a hollow to make a lighter cast.

The plaster goes through a chemical change as it dries, getting hot as it strengthens. It will be brittle at this stage so leave it to cool. You can test whether it has properly hardened by dragging a finger nail across it. If it leaves a mark you must wait a little longer. Only when it is firm enough not to mark should you take the mould from the bowl.

Lay the towel or cloth on the table to provide a surface on which the mould will not slip and turn it over and lay it down with the plaster below.

Now start to remove the bandages. [20] A blunt knife or similar tool may be helpful in doing this but be careful not to damage the plaster face you have cast. The

Make a shrunken face
If you are in no hurry and can leave alginate and mother case together to dry out for four or five days the alginate will shrink and leave you with a mould from which you can cast a shrunken face with perfect little features!

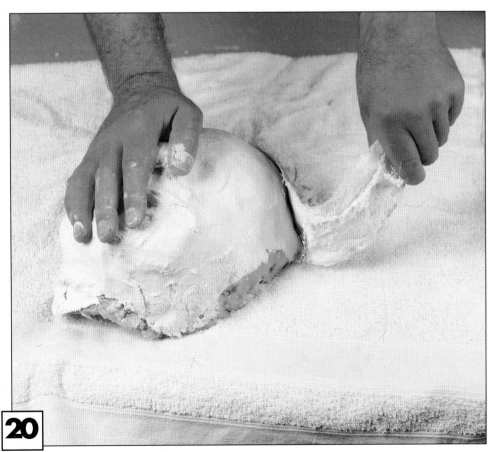

20

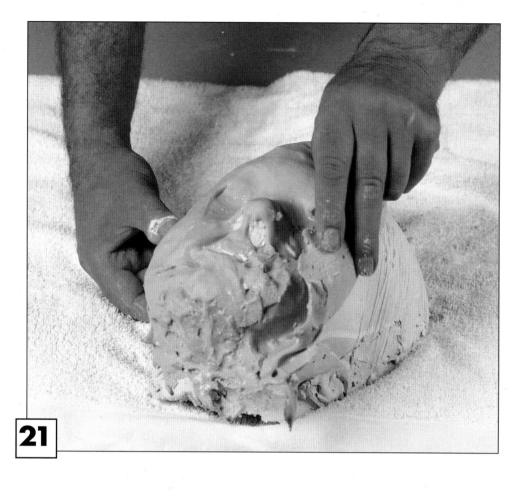

21

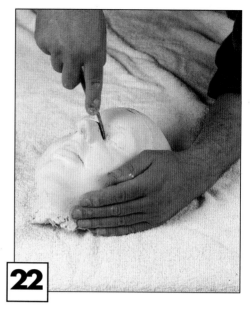

22

alginate will usually come away easily or can just be torn away. [21]

Finishing off

You now have a plaster cast of your subject's face. It will probably have some imperfections. Minor lumps and blemishes can be removed with a wooden tool which will not scratch the surface, though a metal one may be necessary for larger lumps [22]. The nostrils can be made good and eyebrows, beards etc can be carefully carved off with a pocket knife. Go slowly and take care. It is much harder to put back than to gouge away!

The areas usually demanding most care are the pocket in the eye, the lips and sometimes under the chin – though these will be less of a problem in proportion to the care you took in applying the alginate and in filling the mould.

Finally use a power file or a hand rasp to tidy up the outside edge of the cast [23] and give the surface a couple of coats of shellac to seal it. Your face casts now complete. [24]

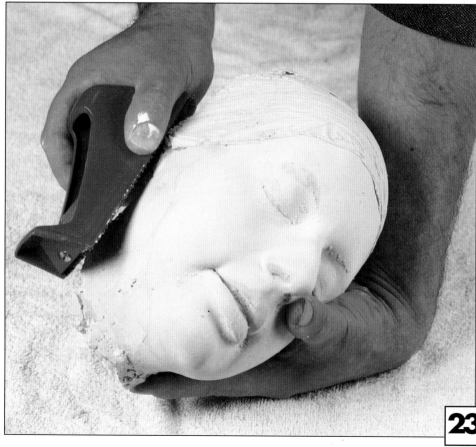

23

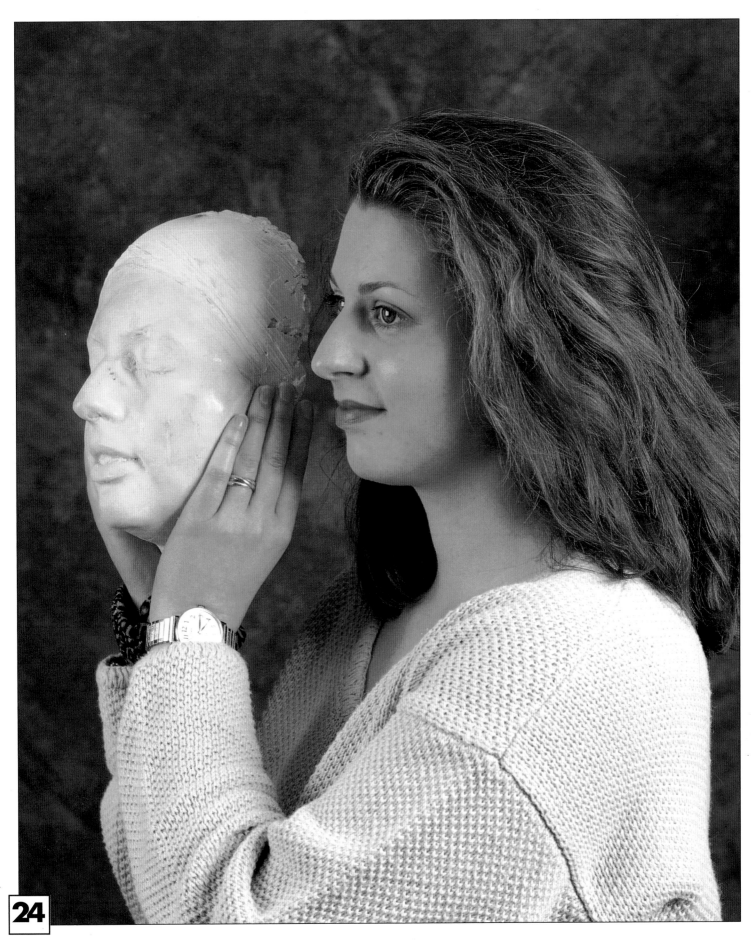

MAKING A SIMPLE SCULPT OVER THE CAST

To make a mask of a different contour from the face of the wearer, but which will be light in weight and still fit comfortably on that face, it is necessary to model the new features. This is done by building up a sculpture in clay on top of a cast made as described in the previous chapter. If a portrait cast of the wearer is not available chose from previously cast faces trying to match width, length and eye and nose positions.

To make a realistic mask of any human or animal form good visual reference is essential. For stage and film work a designer may provide design sketches for you to follow but a collection of your own reference material will be invaluable. Make up a scrap book of pictures from magazines and newspapers and your

MATERIALS NEEDED

Face cast (ideally of wearer)
Water clay or Plasticine
White spirit
Water spray (the kind used for misting plants)
Modelling tools:
Flexible steel scraper (`kidney')
Wire ended modelling tool
Boxwood modelling tool
Sponge

own photographs and organise it under types and subjects. You will want all types and ages of human heads, and animals too. Your mask-making may need references for human injuries and deformities, supernatural beings and characters

from science fiction. Keep an eye open for sources which show details of wrinkles, jowls and individual features which you might wish to copy. Some mask makers even start a collection of casts from live subjects of such details.

Preparation
Prepare a worktop with plenty of working space and good natural light if possible. Protect the floor around with newspapers or plastic sheet. It is surprising how much clay travels around on the soles of shoes and then grinds itself into the carpet. If you are working at home it may be worth wearing old shoes and taking them off before going elsewhere in the house.

Lay out your tools and materials and any reference pictures from which you intend to work.

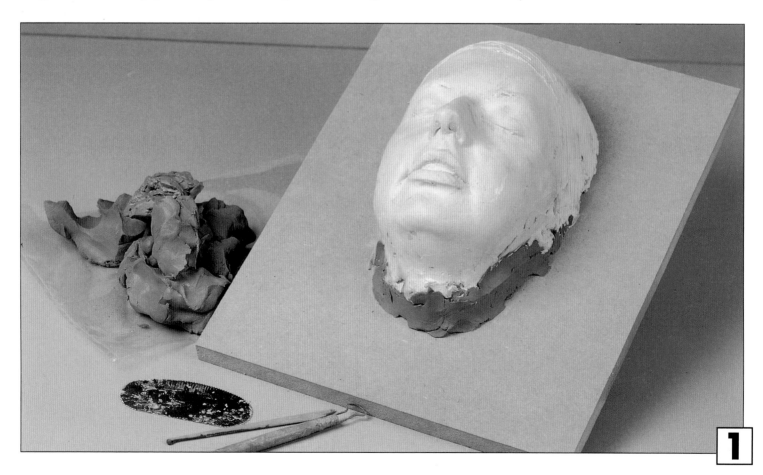

1

There are two types of modelling clay, one based on oil the other on water. Wet clay must be protected from drying. Oil-based, such as the well known Plasticine, has the advantage of not drying out over long periods but is more expensive. Sculptors' suppliers may stock more expensive proprietary brands, such as the French Plastillina, which are easier to use, of different softness and come in various colours.

Take clay out of its pack only as you need it to prevent drying out. Spray with a little water if clay becomes too dry but be careful not to overdo it.

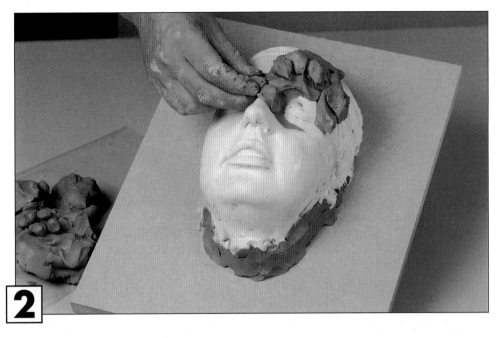

2

Set up the face cast on a firm surface and at a slight angle to the table. [1] If you are making many masks it is worth constructing a stand that can be used every time but you can improvise with a smooth board with a support under one end.

Now sit and take some time to study the face in front of you. Note any sharp features, any undercuts that may get trapped in the mould you will later make. It may help to make a sketch or diagram of what you want to achieve. Remember that in nature the two sides of the face are rarely identical and a very slight variation may create a better effect.

While working on the mask always remember its purpose, how it will be worn and how it is to fit. Never forget that the wearer needs to

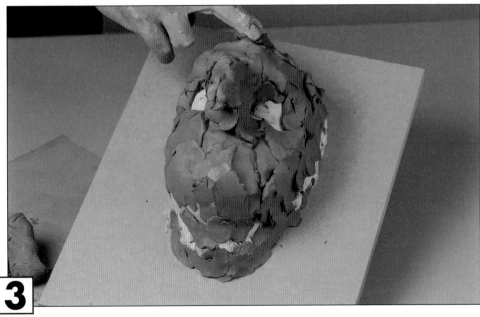

3

Make a stand from a board about 14 in x 22 in (35 x 55 cm) and fix ledges of 2 x 1 in (5 x 2.5 cm) wood on one end of the top face and the other end of the bottom face. One will hold your work, the other stop the stand from slipping when propped over a support. If you use pegboard or lay pegboard over the stand you can fit dowels into the holes around the piece you are working on to prevent sideways movement.

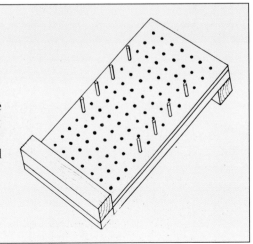

breath, see, hear and probably speak.

Starting the sculpt

Take clay or plasticine in small pea-sized blobs and start applying it to the cast. [2] (If using clay wet the cast first, it helps the clay to adhere. At this stage make no attempt at details but roughly build up the basic muscle shapes. Work on developing the underlying forms.[3]

As the sculpture builds up consider the thickness of your clay. If it is to be a close fitting mask you need only add enough to overcome any

Sculpting tools

Most modelling is done with the fingers and palms of the hands. However small sculpting tools are helpful in refining the details. A wide range of modelling tools are available in both wood and metal and dental tools are also useful for small detail and scraping the harder plasters.

Tools can be pressed into the clay, used to scoop out a shape, drawn along to make a regular curve or undercut. Wire ended tools are effective to cut grooves and channels because they do not push up clay in front of them but cut through the clay.

Thin, flexible metal scrapers are available in both rectangular and kidney shapes, sometimes with toothed edges which can be used to create striated patterns.

Sponges can be used for smoothing down and modelling fluid shapes (muscles or jowls) or rough sponges to add texture. Rubber stamps can be used for textures, lolly sticks, pencils, flexible rulers and paper clips and many more readily available objects can be used as pushing, scraping or marking tools to add to the manufactured ones.

a A wire ended tool is used to carve out small gouges from the clay: it takes away clay depending on the size and outline of the wire.
b Boxwood tools usually have some sort of point at one end (this is used to poke into areas that are inaccessible to the finger) and rounded shapes at the other that can be used to make indentations or smooth small awkward areas.
c The steel kidney is a flexible scaper used mainly for smoothing large areas. Those with a serated edge can be used to show the contours of a sculp before smoothing over.

undercuts and will not build out far from the face. If it is a large animal mask but is still to make contact with the upper face rather than being supported on a headpiece add little to that area (or consider using other materials as described later).

Adding detail

When you are satisfied with the general shape start putting in the detail. [4] Smooth the clay surface by sponging on a little water [5] – use a brush with white spirit if you are working with Plasticine. Do not use much solvent or the sculpt will become sloshy.

Up till now you have probably found it easier to work with the fingers than to use modelling tools but in creating detail they will probably be helpful, especially if you want hard lines and sharp edges.

Always relate the detail of the sculpt to the method and materials to be used in making the mask. If it is to be built up in *papier mâché* or Celastic (a plastic material discussed in a subsequent chapter) or the final finish to the mask is to be done after it has been moulded, there is no point in adding fine detail and texture to your sculpt. However, if the final mask is to be made from latex which will hold very fine detail, even individual pores, you can create detailed textures and wrinkles. Rather than make every mark individually you can make up a stamp to use over textured areas.

Existing details on other life casts or from cloth, or the surfaces of oranges, avocados and other fruit can be useful for creating detail and texture. If you want the finished surface to have the pore-like indentations of, for instance, orange peel, make a stamp by coating a piece of peel with four or five layers of latex. Dry it and powder the surface with talc so that it does not adhere to your clay and peel it away. You can use it again and again.

If you are working with wet clay you may need to let it dry out a little before you are able to add detail – and for very fine detail it may need to be almost hard. However, drying too quickly can cause cracking. Prevent this

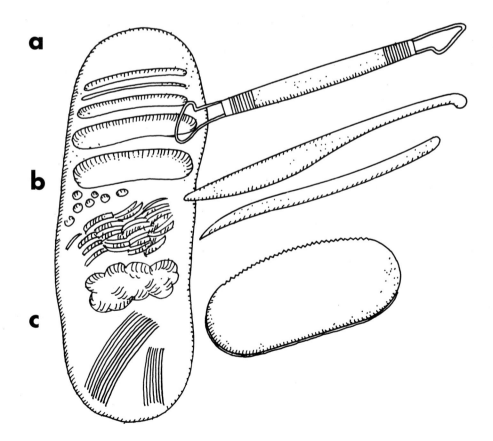

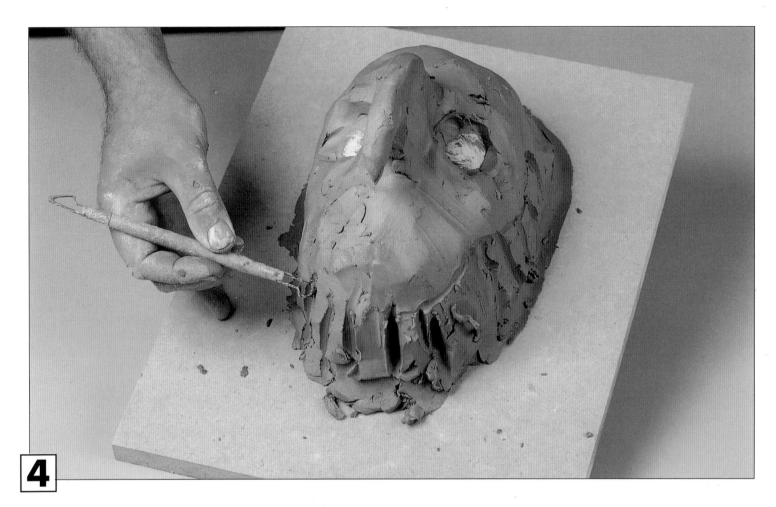

4

by loosely covering it with a polythene bag or a damp cloth.

WARNING:

You will either be making a mould from this sculpt or creating a mask in contact with it. Unless this is a `one-off` and you do not mind the later process destroying your sculpt, you must avoid any `undercutting`, hollows which are narrower near the surface, or indentations in a reverse direction from the main plane of the surface which would make it difficult to lift the contact layer clear.

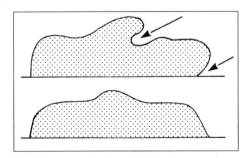

Undercut: the mould will not come off.
No Undercut: the mould will seperate easily.

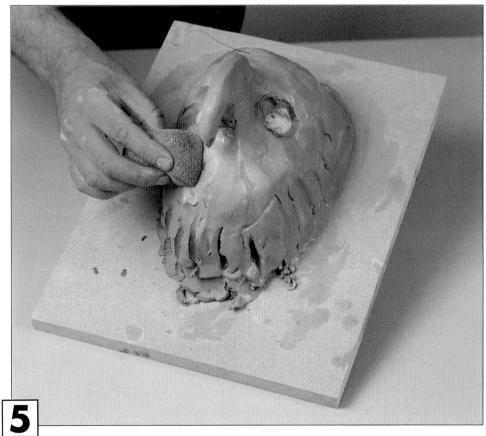

5

MAKING A MASK OVER THE SCULPT FROM PAPER AND GLUE

This is one of the simplest forms of mask making. However, these masks are strictly `one-offs' and repeat masks will not only have to be individually created but require resculpting the features in the clay for they are easily damaged or destroyed in the making and removal of the mask.

It is not a suitable method for masks with undercut features or requiring very fine detail. For them use one of the moulded methods.

The material used to make this mask is a variation on *papier mâche'*– French for chewed-up paper. It has been used for making trays and even furniture and the combination of paper and glue which is easily mould-ed when wet dries to give a light but strong structure. The Roman legionaries wore an armour of a simi-lar material consisting of flax impregnated with glue. *Papier mâche'* sometimes involves paper mixed with a liquid adhesive to form a pulp or by soaking strips of paper in glue and using it in a mould, but here it is built up layer by layer.

Most types of paper can be used: newspaper, kitchen roll, paper napkins – anything which is relatively absorbent, but papers with a hard or coated surface which resists water penetration should be avoided. Acid free paper is preferable. Thin fabrics such as muslin can be incorporated.

Similarly the glue used may be anything from flour paste (safest when very young children are making *papier mâche'*) or cellulose wallpaper paste to glue made from bones. The latter (which has to be cooked up in a glue-pot) makes a hard rigid mask. Wallpaper paste and PVA (polyvinyl acetate) water-based glue dry to a softer finish but are much more convenient.

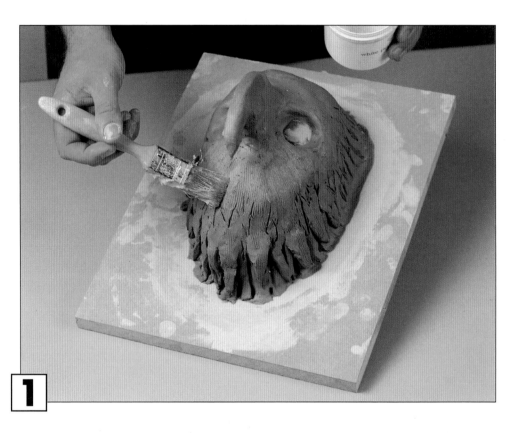

1

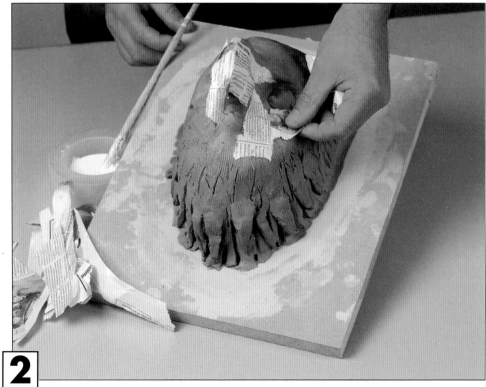

2

Preparation

Tear up paper into strips. Mix up paste or glue. If they are still to hand it is easier to work with the sculpt set over the face cast and on the stand you used to support the cast when making it. Otherwise you will need to arrange support beneath your sculpt.

Use your fingers or a brush to smear petroleum jelly over the surface of the sculpt. [1] This will make it easier to remove the finished mask.

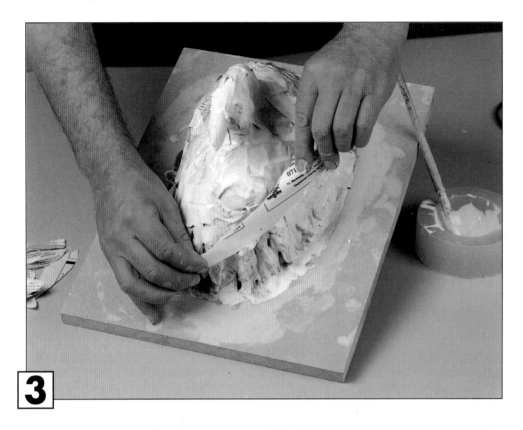

3

Building the mask

Lay strips of paper over your sculpt, close together but without overlapping – the petroleum jelly will help them to stay in place, pressing them neatly into all the detail. [2] You will not get as sharp a result as with a mould but careful application will make a big difference to how much detail is retained. Now apply glue all over them with the paint brush. Use a stipple action in the cracks. Now apply another layer in the opposite direction to the first. [3] Apply glue again and repeat for several layers to strengthen the mask [4], always changing the direction of the lay.

Tear up the paper into smaller pieces if it does not follow the forms easily. The optimum thickness is difficult to judge. About eight layers is usually about right.

If you wish to incorporate a tape for tying around the head into the fabric of the mask lay this across the whole mask after the fourth layer with sufficient length beyond the temple to reach to the back of the head and tie in a bow (or use a Velcro tape).

Leave the mask overnight to dry off. However, it is probably better to leave it on the sculpt until you have finished it.

4

Use two different colours of paper or one plain one printed and change paper when you start each new layer. This will help you build up an even thickness over the mask.

5

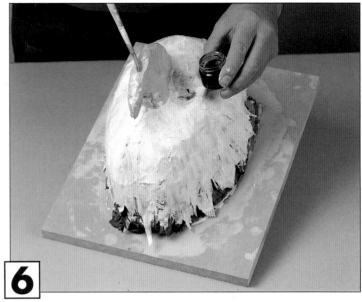

6

Finishing the mask

You can use all kinds of paints, inks and varnishes to create natural features or other decoration and colour can also be built into the mask by using coloured paper or material for the last layer. Thin cloths, gold leaf and other such materials can also be applied. If you are using water paints they must be applied *before* removing the mask from the sculpt as the water may soften the glue.

If you are using transparent colours it is necessary to obscure the colour of the paper and any printing on it by applying a ground colour,

such as a white emulsion paint or acrylic gesso. [5]

A French enamel varnish gives a brilliant iridescent finish and increases the durability of the surface. [6] Building up washes of colour in the varnish will increase the tonal interest and when shades from the same part of the spectrum are mingled gives added vitality. [7]

The dry mask should come away from the sculpt with little difficulty but take great care if you want to to make a duplicate mask for any damage to the sculpt will have to be repaired.

Trim the edge to a neat line with scissors or a craft knife [8]. If you have not already incorporated a tape in the mask, attach a Velcro or elastic headband with a glue gun or staples. Alternatively pierce a hole on either side, reinforce it (this is best done before you finish the decoration) and tie your fastenings through these.

It is not usually necessary to line a light mask of this kind but clean off the Vaseline from the inside with a cloth and surgical spirit if available, then powder with talc to take away any residual stickiness. Do NOT use water.

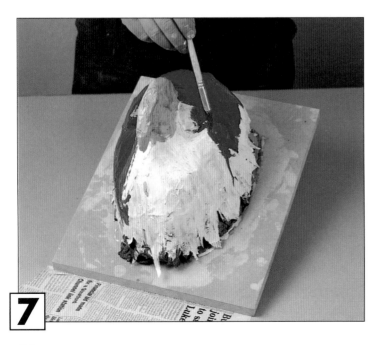

7

8

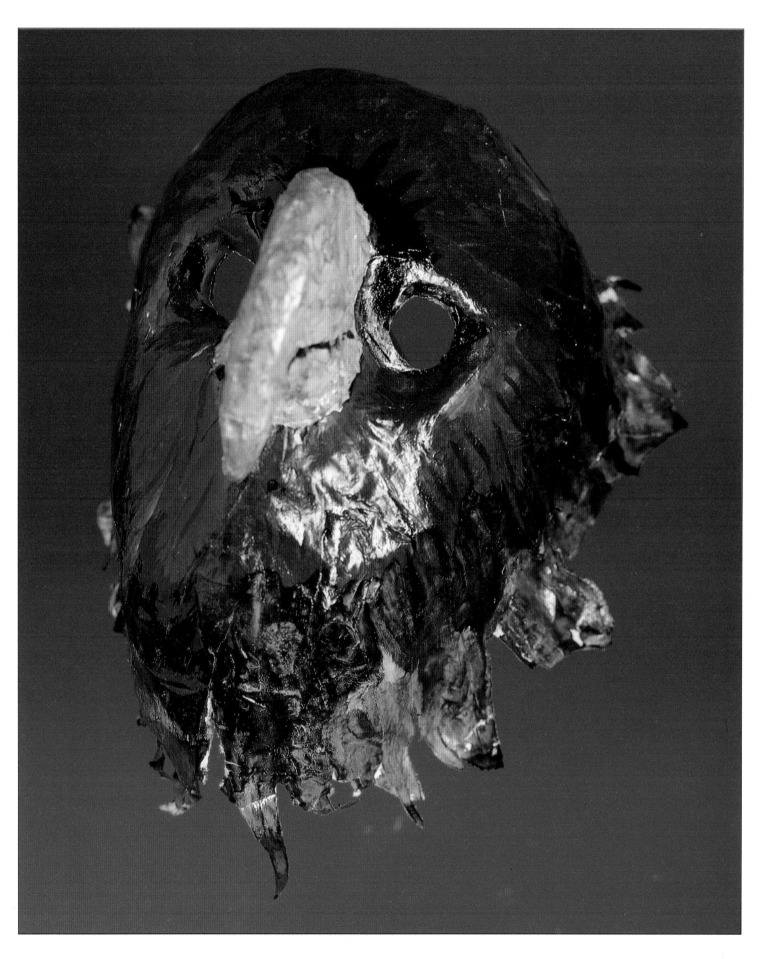

More masks made over a sculpt

A frog mask made over a clay sculpt but, to save time, using plaster bandage (as in the mask made on the face pages 10-14), not paper. The paper mask was coated with rubber-based glue (Copydex) and stockinet stretched over it concealing any blemishes in the surface. This was then covered with a coat of latex to strengthen it and fill in some of the texture and the mask painted and decorated. The result is a heavier mask than more conventional methods but it was finished within one hour!

This mask was for static use and no eye holes were required, but they could have been disguised as nostrils.

A lion mask made by applying strips of Celastic (see pages 48-53) over a plaster cast. You do not always have to make a fresh clay sculpt. The base for this was in fact a garden ornament and any carved or moulded head or face of the right size could be utilized if the surface will not be damaged by working over it and a suitable separator is used. Undercuts in a carving could make it difficult to remove the finished mask so fill them in with clay before beginning your mask and at the same time make good any chips or missing pieces.

The surface of this mask was finished off with flock – the same material as is sometimes used on wallpaper. It comes in a variety of colours (which can be mixed to vary tone and get a special effect) and is simply sprinkled over a wet glued surface. An old wig and a piece of furnishing fringe finished off the mask. The wearer made up round the eyes with black to match the mask.

A giraffe's head, build up over a clay sculpt with paper and glue – in this case wood glue for added strength. Coloured tissue paper was used for the final layer and a gold pigment mixed with PVA glue was used for the horns and tongue.

It is difficult to remove all the clay from long projections such as the horns on this mask but a little left behind will do no harm provided it does not increase the weight too much. Alternatively, horns could be made in other material and glued in place.

When designing animal masks modifications often have to be made if they are to fit over a human face. Here the giraffe's long neck is not attempted. A long-necked mask could be constructed, with a vision panel set into the neck, but this would require the construction of a framework to carry the structure.

A vulture mask made over a clay sculpt with muslin and PVA glue. This produced a very lightweight mask. Most birds have their eyes set much further to the sides than those of humans so they could not be used to see through. Although the head has been somewhat humanised, the lower mandible being treated more like a jaw and a strong eyebrow line included, both helping to add to the characterisation, the eyes and beak emphasise the vulturine features. The bird's nostrils, though not placed anatomically correctly, enable to wearer to see out. It is not an ideal solution for the protruding beak produces tunnel vision but the alternative of hiding holes under fine net would have met the same problem. Feathers supplied in a continuous string have been glued on to form the ruff.

MAKING A SIMPLE PLASTER MOULD

The object here is to make a mould from the sculpted face so that it can be reproduced in other materials and in multiples, retaining finer details than are possible with the preceding type of mask.

For most types of mould, plaster of Paris is adequate but there are other materials available which are stronger and more durable or which are suitable when you wish to dry latex in an oven or bake foam rubber.

MATERIALS NEEDED

Sculpt of mask for casting mould
Plaster
Clay
Petroleum jelly (Vaseline)
   or Talcum powder,
   soap or wax polish
Flexible bowls
Spray on furniture polish
Base board with Formica surface
   (or covered with polythene)
1 in (2.5 cm) soft-bristled paint
   brush
Plaster knife or pocket knife
Rasp

Preparations

Protect your work surface and working area from plaster splashes and lay out your tools and materials.

Flexible bowls enable you to crack out dry plaster after use but you can make cleaning after use even easier by spraying the inside of bowl with furniture polish, which helps to prevent plaster from sticking.

Your sculpt over a face mask will still be on its base board. If you are making the mould directly after finishing the sculpt, clay will still be wettish. If it has dried out, then a light application of a separator such as petroleum jelly will do no harm.

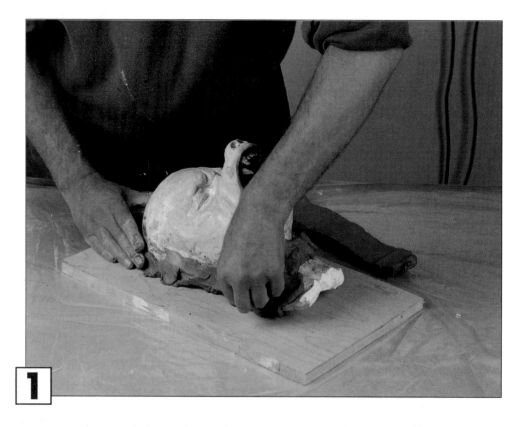

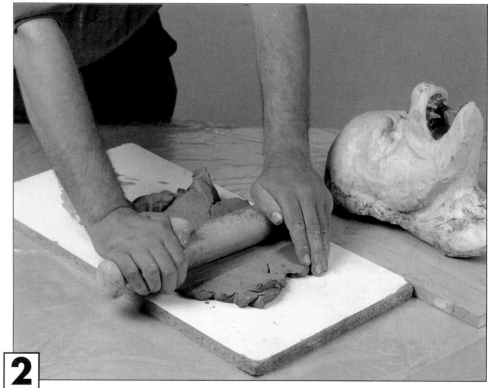

Set a band of wet clay beneath the sculpt to seal it to the board and so prevent plaster from running underneath it. [1]

Roll out a slab of clay like pastry, using a rolling pin or a bottle, to produce an even thickness. [2] Use this slab to build up a substantial wall of clay all around the sculpt and about 2 in (5 cm) distant from it. [3] Alternatively, bend a piece of card to make the wall and fix it down with clay. The card should be sufficient for a simple mould, for bigger and complex pieces use all clay.

Apply petroleum jelly to the eyes and any areas of the plaster face cast which have not been covered by clay or Plasticine. [4]

Now you are ready to mix the plaster as described on pages 24-25. Most plasters are mixed in the same way, except for dental stone which comes in cans and requires careful measuring to get the right consistency. Check the manufacturers instructions carefully when using the more sophisticated plasters.

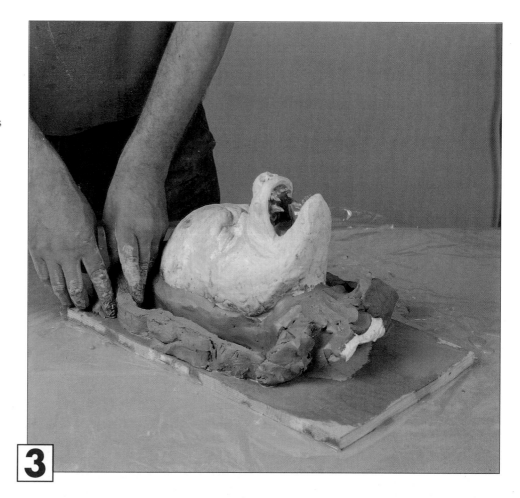

3

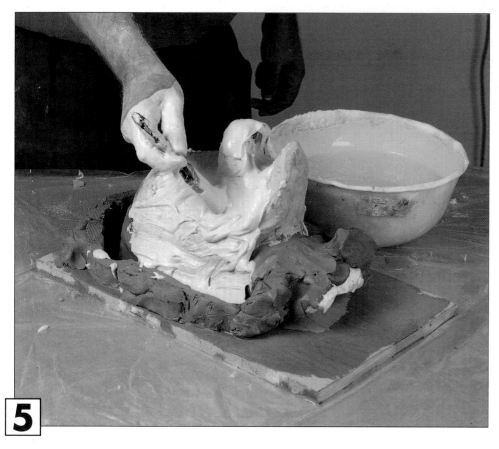

5

4

Making the mould

When the plaster is ready for use begin to pour it into the well between the wall you have built and the sculpt. Quickly check for leaks around the wall and plug any with more clay before proceeding. Now rub a paintbrush on a wet piece of soap or rub a drop of washing up liquid over it (this will make it easier to clean later) then load it with plaster and gently brush a first coat over your sculpt, making sure that it fills all the detail. [5] Go on building up the rest. As the plaster begins to `go off' you can draw

39

up more over the top. [6] You need to build up a thickness of 1-1.5 in (2.5-3.75 cm).

If you do this correctly there should be no need for reinforcement except on larger pieces (in which case follow the instructions given on page 70 for two part moulds).

WARNING:
Wash the plaster out of your paintbrush as soon as you have finished using it or it will be ruined.

Leave the plaster as it makes its chemical change, becomes hot and then starts to cool. If it has properly hardened a fingernail dragged across the back should leave no mark.

As it cools remove the clay wall and loosen the mould from the base. Extracting the clay from the mould is easier during this final cooling period than when the mould is completely dry. [7] Plasticine is harder to remove as it has melted from the heat produced. If there are places where it is stuck you may find using a wooden

6

modelling tool will help to draw it out – but do not use a metal object or you will damage the plaster. Stubborn clay can be wetted and washed out.

Carefully trim the edges with a plaster knife or a penknife and remove any sharp projections from the outer surface with the rasp. [8] Now leave it to dry out completely. Do not try to mould from it for at least half an hour.

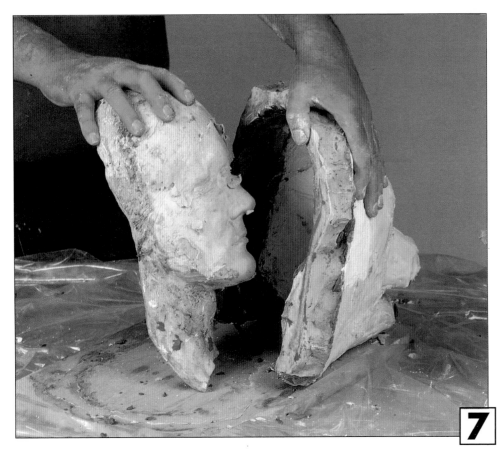

7

8

40

MAKING A LATEX MASK

Natural latex is the sap exuded from the rubber tree. Water and ammonia are added to it to stop it from coagulating and since ammonia will irritate the skin it is preferable to wear rubber gloves to work with it. If you do handle it in direct contact with the skin then make sure that the hands are thoroughly washed with soap in warm water afterwards.

Latex is supplied in several forms. Thin, runny latex can be used to form a thin, soft and skin-like flexible mask. This relies on the face inside to support it or requires a polyurethane foam former, or Celastic or cut sponge support.

Latex with a filler (such as Protex) is thickened by the addition of clay and can be used to make a rigid or semi-rigid mask, depending on thickness, which allows you to make large projections such as long noses and horns.

Both kinds of latex can be coloured by the addition of water colour. The amount of pigment is difficult to judge and you may have to make several tests to get the effect you want. It is easier to colour the finished mask.

1

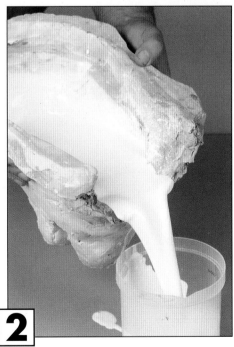

2

MATERIALS NEEDED

Plaster mould
Latex (runny) for thin masks
Latex with filler for thick
   contours
Soft paintbrush
Soap

Preparation

If the mould is an old one that has dried out give it a soak in water to dispel any air within it. If it is one that has only just been cast the warmth still retained within it will speed the drying of the latex.

Set the mould up with a support around it to make it stable.

Rub the bristles of the brush on to some wet soap. This will make it easier to wash out afterwards.

Now you can open your latex container. Keep it close to the mould to avoid drips.

Using the mould

Latex is very easy to use, but chose the type which is best suited to the type of mask you are making.

Begin by pouring a little into your mould and then brush it into the detail. **[1]**

If you are using latex with filler, once the surface is covered you can top up the mould by pouring latex in. Leave it for 10 minutes and then pour latex from the mould back into the container. **[2]**

Check that the thickness of the build is sufficient for your needs and top up with a little more and repeat until you have the thickness you require. Do not allow it to dry out between pourings or the next fill will not adhere.

For a flexible mask simply brush in more layers of latex until a satisfactory thickness is achieved. The moisture in the latex is absorbed into the plaster, drying it.

Both kinds of latex can be reinforced by laying a piece of stocking or even hessian in the layers, especially in the temple area where the ties will be attached.

You can speed the drying of the flexible mask by blowing on it with a hand-held hair-dryer. Even when it is dry, if you feel a flexible latex mask is too thin, you can brush on further layers of latex.

The latex with filler must either be left to dry for at least 24 hours at room temperature or have its drying speeded up in a cool oven set to not more than 225 ° F (110 °C) or Gas Mark 1/4. Allow about two hours in the oven, but check well before, the time required will vary according to the density of the mask.

If, during the removal of the mask, you get any talcum powder into the mould wash it out with soap and water and a soft brush. If any remains it will cause separation and the latex will not hold to the sides of the mould when it is next used.

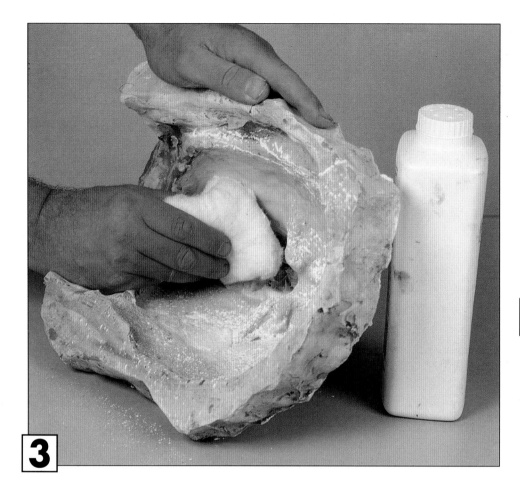

3

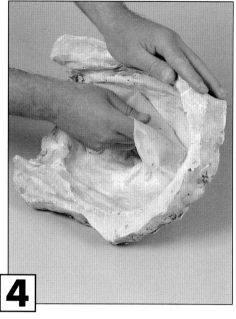

4

with a glue gun or with staples.

Now you can paint the mask. It takes two to three days to completely harden, but you should paint it as soon as possible after taking it from the mould, when the colours are absorbed better by the latex. Just make

When the latex is dry, powder the whole thing to prevent it sticking to itself [3] and remove gently from the mould. [4] [5] The latex with filler is sometimes harder to remove, especially if the mould has deep nostrils, jowls etc, but simply reshape it with your fingers if the mask became distorted and set it aside to dry out further.

Finishing the mask

Lining latex masks is not usual, how-ever, masks of the harder type can be made more comfortable by applying small pieces of suede as described in the next chapter for celastic masks.

Cut around the perimeter of the mask itself with sharp scissors. [6] If you need to trim eye holes use a craft knife – and take care, it is a tricky job and if the knife slips you could ruin the mask and give yourself an injury.

Strips of Velcro or bands to tie the mask onto the head can be attached to the edges of the mask, either by gluing

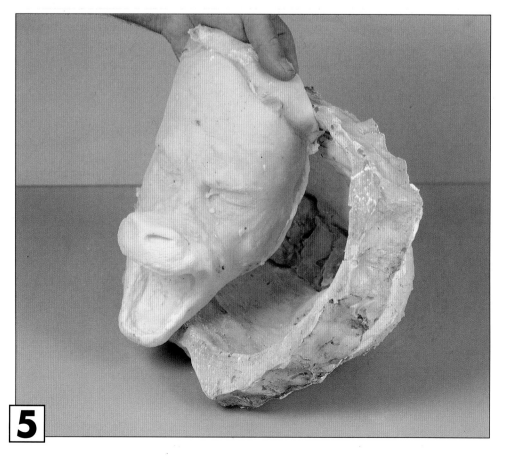

5

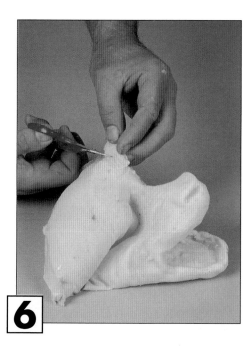

6

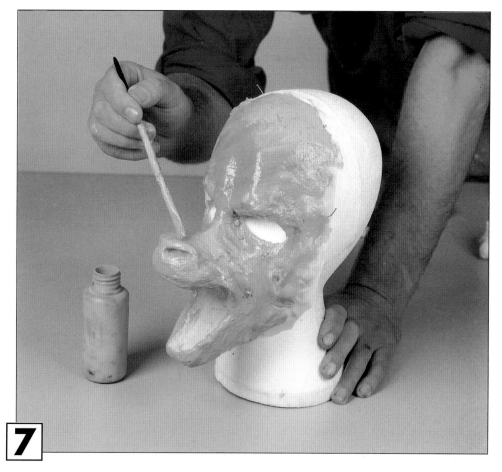

7

sure the latex is firm enough not to be distorted by your brushwork. Set the mask over a head block or a full head cast (see pages 66-67) to make this job much easier. [7]

Overall colour could have been added to the latex prior to moulding

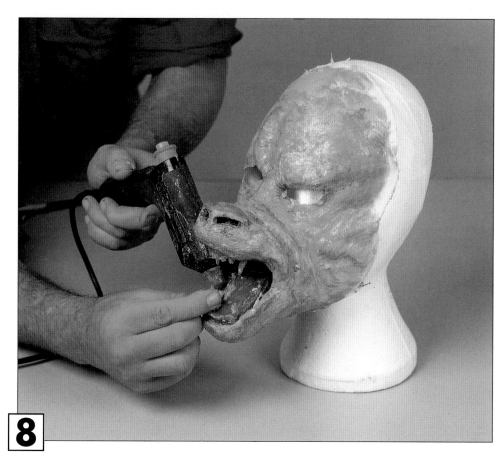

8

but the surface can now be painted with inks, watered acrylic paint or (the author's favourite) coloured hair sprays. The options are many but the paint must remain flexible so that it does not crack when the mask moves.

Additions not included in the sculpt, such as the precast tongue and teeth (see pages 54-60) which have been made separately, can now be fixed in place using a hot glue gun. [8] Hair and other details finally complete the mask, which is at last revealed as a Werewolf! [overleaf]

Masks moulded from latex:
A werewolf mask, the making of which is described on the preceding pages. Precast teeth and tongue have been set in place and the addition of a wig completes the creature's character.

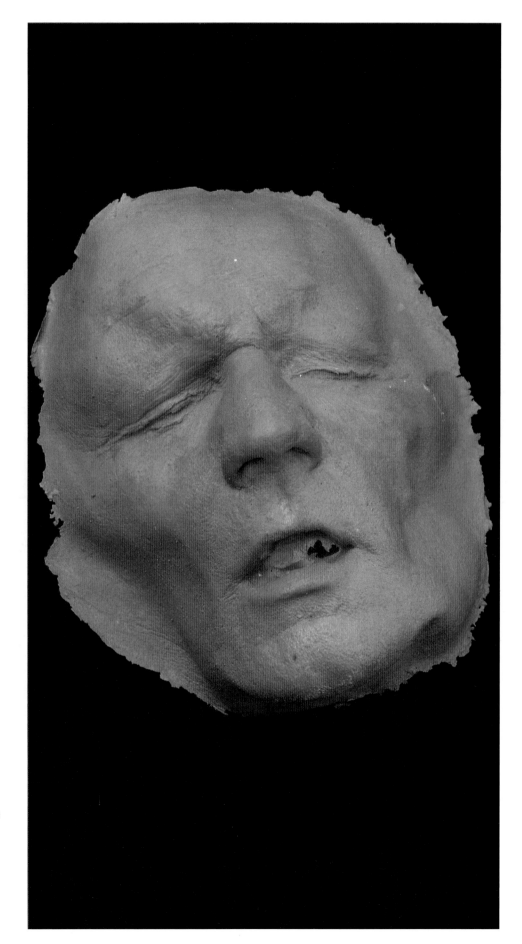

This mask was made from a life cast of a human face. Instead of filling the alginate mould with plaster to make a face cast molten wax was poured in. When this wax had set it was removed. The wax face was then covered with plaster of Paris to give a plaster mould of the face. From this the latex mask was cast,

It was a relatively simple mask to paint, adding colour while the latex was still absorbent. The mouth still has to be finished, cutting away spare latex with a knife, but in this case the mask was to be removed during the action revealing the actor's real face beneath and the eyelids were left intact. If the eye sockets in the mould had been carefully smeared with petroleum jelly before the latex was poured in this would have left appropriate holes in the latex mask.

A monkey mask, actually made as a whole head in a two-part mould (as described in the final chapter) but the face could easily have been cast alone. The subject is so close to the human that the challenge here is to get the sculpt just right. To make it look more real the painting used water shades painted over each other. Latex with filler was used here to ensure the mask keeps its form. Shades of different yak hair were mixed to avoid the deadness of plain black hair.

Dog masks moulded from latex with a filler. The ears were made flatter than usual to make it easier to remove them from the mould and their backs were carefully levelled with the front so that when the latex was poured the ears would fill without leaving a point for the latex to run out. These masks fit closely to the face and could equally well have been moulded in ordinary latex to provide flexible jowls.

MAKING A CELASTIC MASK

Celastic ia a material impregnated with plastic which softens when immersed in acetone and hardens when left to dry again. One of its uses was in shoemaking. It is available in three different thicknessess. All thicknesses are of use in mask making but the middle one offers a combination of strength and ease in moulding.

Preparation

Clear an uncluttered worktop and set out your tools and materials.

Tear a sheet of Celastic into strips 1-2 in (2.5-5cm) wide and then tear them again into lengths of about 6 in (15cm). Do NOT cut them, tearing feathers the edges and makes better blends in the mould. However, if you have difficulty in ripping them cut a nick at regular intervals along the edge to give you a start. Keep these together in a box. If you don't use them all they are ready for another day.

Use the paintbrush to coat the inside of the mould with petroleum jelly. (A special separator is available from suppliers of Celastic but this does the job just as well.) [1]

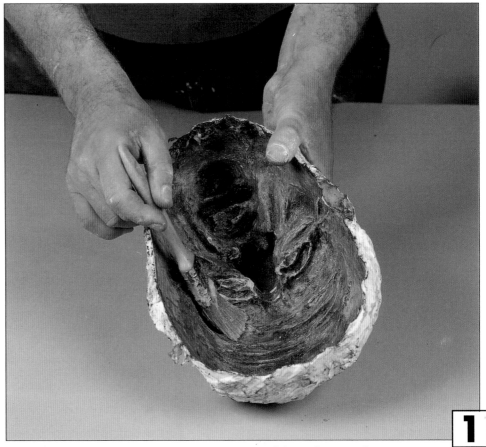

1

NOW PUT ON YOUR GOGGLES AND SAFETY MASK AND THEN YOUR RUBBER GLOVES.

Making the mask

Open the acetone and pour a little into the glass, ceramic or polythene

---

MATERIALS NEEDED

Mould
Celastic
Acetone
Petroleum jelly (Vaseline)
Paint
Cellulose filler

Modelling medium (such as Das or Milleput)
Rubber-based adhesive (Copydex)
Ceramic or glass bowl
A cardboard or plastic box to hold torn Celastic
Fine wet/dry sandpaper
1in (2.5 cm) paintbrush

Round-ended stick if working in very fine detail
Knife
Scissors
Rubber gloves
Face mask
Goggles
Support for mould if needed

SAFETY PRECAUTIONS

Acetone produces dangerous very flammable fumes. Keep the quantity you use to a minimum. Do NOT put it into plastic containers. NEVER use it in a confined space. KEEP WINDOWS OPEN. Do NOT smoke, eat or drink while working with it. WEAR RUBBER GLOVES. Wear goggles to protect the eyes. If you are going to use acetone for any length of time or use it regularly then invest in a proper face mask, available from sculpting material and fibreglass suppliers.

bowl. It evaporates quickly so don't pour out too much. Recap the container. Take one three-inch (7.5 cm) piece of Celastic and wet it in the acetone. Do not let it soak or the plastic will be washed out of the material. Now lay it in the nose area and gently rub it into the mould with your gloved finger. [2] If some of the details are too fine to get the fingers into then use a round-ended stick or something similar.

Now lay another strip slightly overlapping it, gradually building outwards.

Make sure that the fabric is pressed into all the crevices in the mould. When the mould is covered with one layer begin another, at right angles to the direction of the first layer wherever possible. [3] This strengthens the layer and avoids gaps. With medium-weight Celastic two layers are usually sufficient. They can now be left to dry overnight. If there is any acetone remaining in the bowl pour it into another sealable can for later use. Do NOT pour it down the sink or toilet bowl. Clear up the area carefully. Acetone soaked material is a serious fire risk.

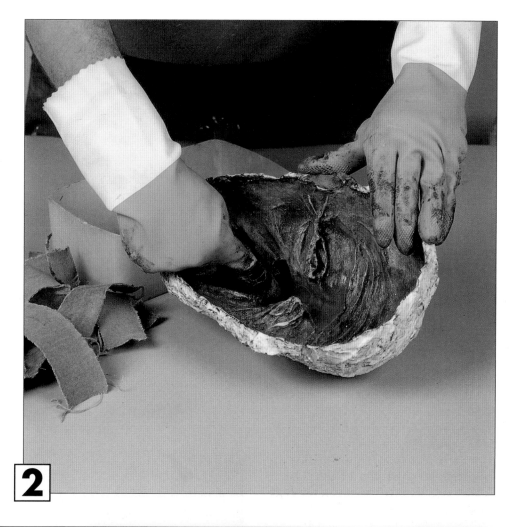

2

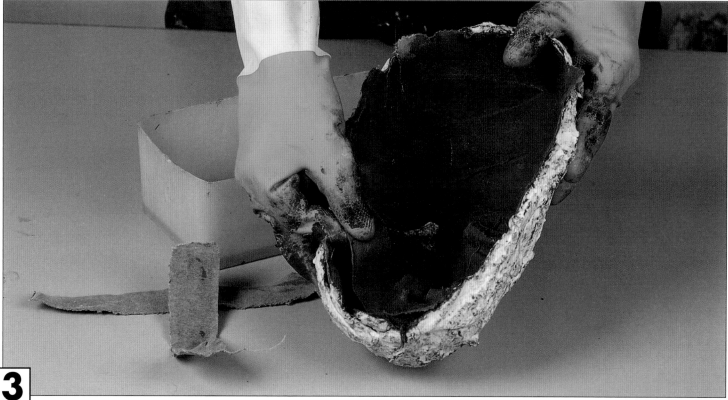

3

4

Removing the mask

When the mask is dry, (it is best left overnight), use a pair of pliers to loosen the edges around the mould. [4] Make sure that you have both layers in their grip before exerting any pressure – you don't want to split the mask! To loosen the mask push and pull with them gently but vigorously,

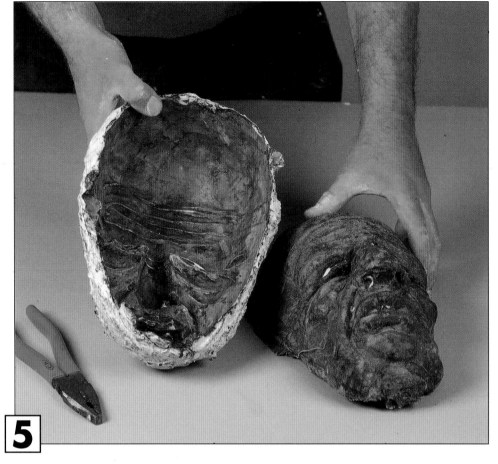

5

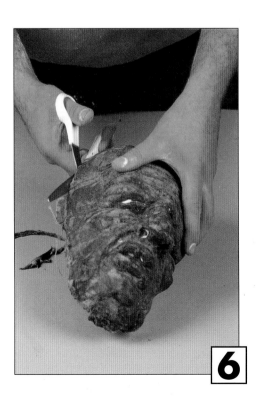

6

7

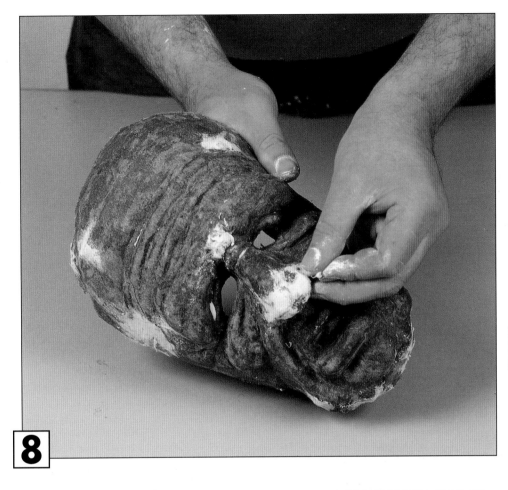

8

10

gradually working all round the edge. Do not give a concentrated pull from one point as this is more likely to cause the mask to tear. If removal does cause any minor damage it can usually be corrected at the next stage.[5]

If some layers are not adhering firmly, stick them together with a rubber adhesive such as Copydex. Do not wet them again with acetone as this make them lose shape.

Trim around the outer edge of the mask with scissors. [6] Use a craft knife to carefully cut out the eye-holes, in this case the eyelid area. [7] Depending on what the use is to be and design requirements, you may need to cut out the mouth and nostrils, or other holes for breathing and ventilation. Any irregularies can be filled with a quick-drying modelling material which can be sanded easily, such as Das or Milleput. [8]

Preparing the finish
Take some ordinary white emulsion paint and mix in about one third volume of pre-wetted cellulose filler (Polyfilla or similar). [9] Paint this over the mask, building up several layers to smooth out he imperfections. [10] After applying each layer use a fine wet-and-dry sandpaper to refine the surface

9

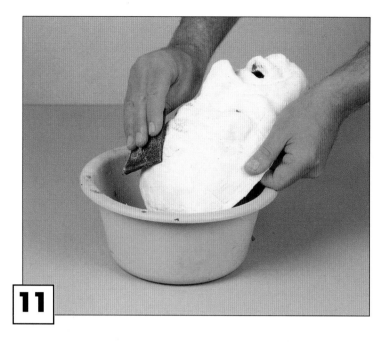

11

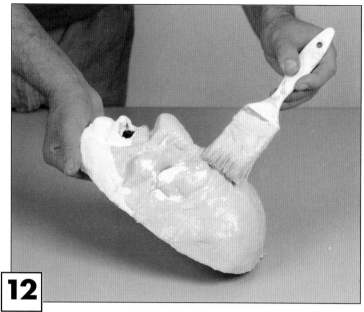

12

before adding another coat until you are satisfied with the finish. [11]

If there are still imperfections fill them with more quick-drying modelling material (Das or Milleput) and smooth over the surface with a damp finger. As soon as this is dry you can begin its decoration.

Decorating the mask

First you must apply a ground coat of appropriate flesh tone or other background colour, using either an emulsion or an acrylic paint. [12] The mask is now ready for you to begin painting in its character features or other decoration, again using emulsion or acrylics. [13]

When you are sure you do not wish to add any further painted features and all the paint is dry, apply a final coat of transparent matt acrylic varnish. This is a pliable varnish which will not crack when the mask moves. It will strengthen the finish and give protection from accidental marking. The mask is now ready for lining.

Lining the mask

Lining the mask not only makes it more comfortable in wear but also makes it easier to clean. Take some wash-leather (chamois) and cut out small pieces fitting them, jig-saw-like, to butt against each other and cover

the back of the mask. By using small pieces you will able to fit them into the contours of the mask without forming creases. Glue them in with a rubber adhesive such as Copydex.

When they are dry trim the edges, including any projecting over the apertures in the mask, with a craft

knife. Attach the mask to its head piece or fix Velcro strips or head bands at the sides of the temples, long enough to meet or tie behind the head.

Hair can now be added (see pages 57-59) if required and the mask is complete, or can be combined with a head piece for a bald effect. [14]

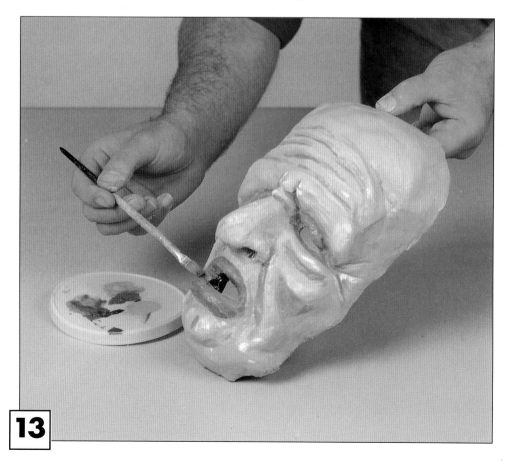

13

14

More Celastic masks:

Masks made for a production of Euripedes' **'Medea'**. No actual Greek or Roman theatre masks survive from ancient times, only a few representations in sculpture, vase paintings and mosaics. We do not even know for certain of what materials they were made. These masks make use of a very contemporary material, Celastic, and do not attempt to copy ancient originals. although their design was influenced by them.

    The mask for the elderly tutor to Medea's children, the making of which is shown on the previous pages, had a Celastic bald pate combined with the mask but these use a separate head piece to which the masks are attached as shown in a later chapter. The mask for Medea herself is used with a wig.

Two masks made in Celastic and strongly influenced by **commedia dell' arte** designs. The intention was to suggest the leather of which the traditional Italian masks were made. They were spray-painted over an undercoat and then given a final finish with a wax shoe polish. The mouth is cut away and the jaw is completely free allowing easy speech and expression with the lips. The nostrils are not cut out because the masks rest on the bridge of the nose, not over its tip, leaving the wearers' airways unobstructed. These masks shows how effectively a simple stylized design establishes character.

Masks can make attractive decorations and this pair of faces, happy and sad, were made for wall mounting and have been joined together. However, each is a complete and practical mask.

They were made in Celastic, though are equally suited to making in latex with filler. They were finished with an acrylic paint, mixing gold and bronze, again using two colours to add more interest to their appearance than a single tone.

CHARACTER ADDITIONS: HAIR, TEETH AND EYES

You do not have to mould every detail of your mask or build it up in the original *papier mâche'*. As well as adding colour to the surface you can incorporate other materials. For instance, only the most stylized hair can be modelled as part of the mask itself and the addition of real or synthetic hair will lift the appearance from the prosaic to the special. Realistic teeth, of a different texture from the `skin' will make it much more real – especially if you want them to look sharp and dangerous. If the wearer does not need to see through the eye sockets, realistic eyes can be inserted. For some creatures you might even want to add a tongue. Ear rings, nose rings and other face jewellery are much better added than attempting to make them as an integral part of the mask.

Hair

Human hair differs considerably, even within the broad types of Chinese, Indian, African and European, and then there are all the other types of animal hair. Real human hair is too expensive and not easy to handle. Yak hair is often used and the writer prefers Yak – but even that is becoming increasingly costly. Fortunately there are very good synthetic alternatives available both in loose hanks and in weft, woven through a narrow braid to form a continuous fringe. There is also theatrical crêpe hair which comes in plaits and has a tight wave when unravelled – it needs dampening and combing if you want to loose the curl.

Of course, if expense is no object you could use already made up wigs, hairpieces, beards and moustaches which have the hair knotted through a gauze base, or have lines of weft sewn onto then, and glue them to your mask, but applying strands directly can be just as effective and is very much cheaper.

When using hair it is best to vary the colour slightly. Unless you are using all black or all white for their particular effect, a single tone looks flat and unnatural. You can dye hair to achieve this difference and may need to if you want unusual colours. Yak hair will dye easily with ordinary dyes made for synthetic fabrics. Hot-water dyes penetrate more readily than the cold-water types.

Boil each hank until the desired strength is achieved and then hang them up to dry.

Mixing hair

You can mix hair by laying hanks of different shades together and holding them in one hand and then pulling them apart with the other, continually returning them to the bundle and repeating the action until you are satisfied with the mix.

It is easiest and much more effective to mix them using a hackle. This is a tool consisting of rows of spikes and originally used for combing out flax or hemp in making thread and string. You could make your own by knocking nails through a piece of wood but it is not easy to drive them all in at a regular angle.

A bought hackle should come with clamps to fix it to your work-surface and a cover to protect you from its sharp spikes when not in use. These are equally necessary if you attempt to make your own. Always take the utmost care when a hackle is uncovered, the rack of sharp points can scratch deeply.

Secure the hackle to your work top by the clamps. Place it to one side so that you will not have to lean over it to work on your mask. Its spikes should point away from you.

To mix hair lay several different shades of hair lengthwise along it, extending about six inches (15 cm) beyond it towards you, taking care not to catch your fingers on its spikes. [1] Pull out a mixture of shades with one hand and gradually build up a bunch of hair in the other hand.

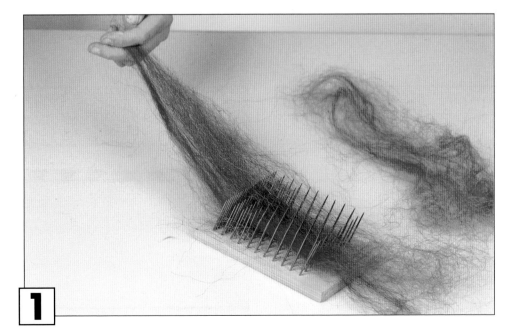

1

Repeat the process two or three times until you are happy with the mix and have as much hair prepared as you expect to need. It is not always easy to match a mixture if you run short.

Now put the hair back on the hackle. Replace the lid to cover the spikes and pull out hair as you need it.

NOTE:
If you use real hair, note that it has a root end and a point end. Always keep the root ends together. If you muddle them up with the point ends the hair will not hang properly but will ride up on itself.

Applying hair

To apply hair you need to support the mask upon a stand. A head block, or a full-head cast (see pages 66-67) are ideal but you can easily adapt a cheap polystyrene head to make a block over which you can slip the mask (see panel on page 60).

The easiest way of fixing hair to your mask is to use a rubber-based adhesive, such as Copydex. Spirit gum is an alternative but it shines unless you use the matt type. In easily manageable areas simply paint the adhesive onto the mask. [2] Apply the hair to it.

For a beard, start under the chin and work upwards. Take out a small clump of hair and holding it between you thumb and forefinger `offer' it to the glue. Use a pair of scissors in the other hand to spread the roots upwards and ensure contact.[3]

Work lightly and horizontally across, then move upwards so that the hair overhangs naturally. [4] If a few hairs do not stick properly ignore them for the moment. Wait until all the hair has been applied and allowed to dry then, holding one hand against the glued ends to avoid more hairs being ripped out, gently tease a broad-toothed comb through the beard.

Adopt the same technique for hair for moustaches, eyebrows and elsewhere. [5] Always work in the direction which allows the overlap to look most natural.

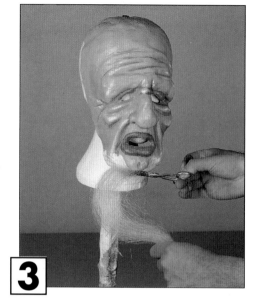

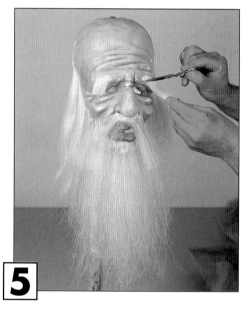

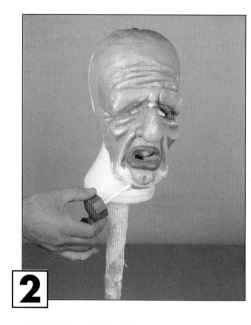

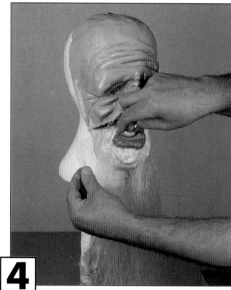

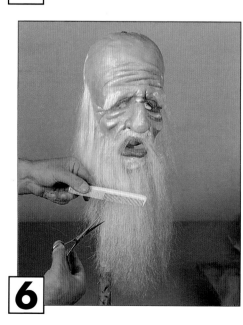

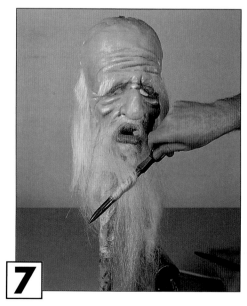

8

perhaps the ideal substance for making them. Its light weight, strength and speed of setting make it also useful for forming eyes and other maskwork – even for making half masks, though perhaps too expensive for extensive use it is a valuable addition to mask-making materials.

Follow the instructions on the packs of these materials. They can be dangerous. Like the acetone used with Celastic and like polyfoam, they are certainly NOT suitable for use by children.

If you wish to use them, for the best effect make a cast from real teeth, or teeth modelled in Plasticine or modelling wax from reference photographs. In animal masks with a structured muzzle and jaw (as for the werewolf mask on page 44) it is easier to mould a whole set. Human masks, which do not attempt to reproduce the complete interior of the mouth usually incorporate a limited number of teeth arranged across the mask. This is best done using individual artificial teeth which which can be pressed into the sculpt to leave cavities into which they can later be inserted.

> **DANGER**
> **When working with acrylic and monomer keep windows wide open. Their fumes are dangerous and flammable. Being heavier than air they will build up at floor level. ALWAYS WEAR PROTECTIVE GLOVES AND GOGGLES.**

Making teeth
Obtain or model teeth, either singly or as a set (in the case of the werewolf the whole palate and tongue were included). [1] overleaf.

Use dental alginate to make a mould. Put the tooth or teeth in a small cardboard or plastic pill box or tub and then pour alginate over them. When the alginate has set [2], the tooth or Plasticine copy will pull out easily. [3] Use the impression it leaves as the mould in which to cast teeth with the acrylic mix.

Trimming hair
If you have never trimmed someone else's hair or beard this takes some getting used to. Use a pair of proper hairdressers scissors if you can. [6] Avoid cutting the hair into `steps' by cutting upwards into it instead of across it.

Curling hair
The easiest way to wave or curl real or artificial hair is to use a pair of curling tongs. [7] These are available with an electric heating element. Old-fashioned ones were pushed into a fire or held over a hot flame. Always test the heat on a piece of paper first. If it scorches more than a very light brown they are too hot.

Take care that you never allow the tongs to make contact with a rubber mask or you could ruin it. To avoid this risk, or if you cannot obtain hot tongs or do not like the idea of using them, wet the hair and put it in rollers. However, this will only put in a basic curl – tongs do much more – and you will still have to take care not to soak the mask and damage it,

When you have finished dressing the hair spray it with a heavy duty hairspray to fix it. [8]

Teeth
Dental material suppliers sell acrylic powder and a monomer which is mixed with it to activate hardening. Used for repairing dentures, this is

Mix the acrylic and polymer in the cut-off bottoms of small polythene containers. [4] If you have modelled a set of teeth set into the gum then make use of the two colours in which it is made. Place the ivory mix into the tooth cavity in the mould. A cocktail stick will be a help in pushing it in and in avoiding air bubbles. [5] Now top up the rest of the mould with the pink mix. [6]

When the mixture has set. carefully pull off the alginate [7] and then file away any jagged bits with a nail file. [8] Paint on water-thinned acrylic paint to give a stained appearance [9] and then a coat of clear nail varnish to give the effect of wet teeth. [10] Glue the finished teeth into cavities moulded in the mask with a glue gun.

An easy alternative, and not as expensive as you may think, is to purchase ready-made teeth from a taxidermy supplier.

Making a simple head block

You will find a head block useful for many processes in mask making and absolutely essential when applying hair. Blocks can be bought from wig makers and millinery suppliers but a cheaper alternative is to buy a polystyrene head and cover it with a fibre-glass or cellulose filler. Cover the base as well as the head itself so that the whole piece is sealed in a coat of filler.

It will take some time to prepare but will save the hobbyist consider-able expenditure.

There are some very good lightweight fillers on the market. Mix them as directed and apply to the head shape as evenly as possible. Then leave it to harden before rubbing it to a smooth finish with wet-and-dry sandpaper.

Because it is so light it is best fixed to a heavy base. A simple method is to spear it on a broom handle and put the other end in a bowl of wet plaster or use an old can and leave the plaster in it.

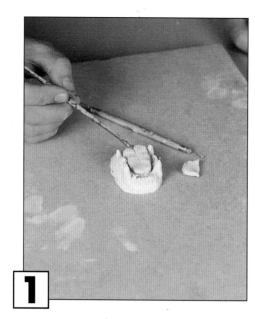

1

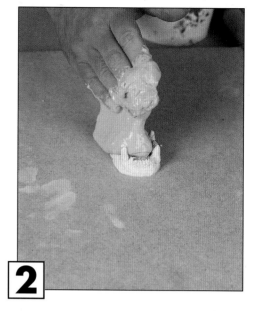

2

3

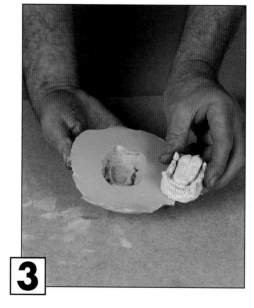

4

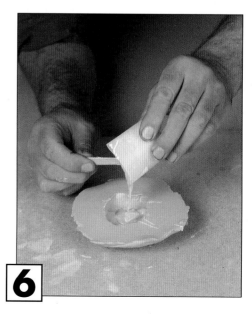

5

6

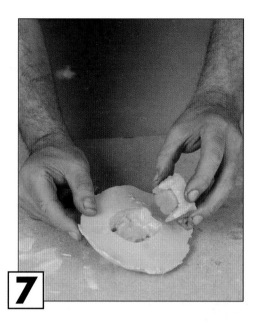

7

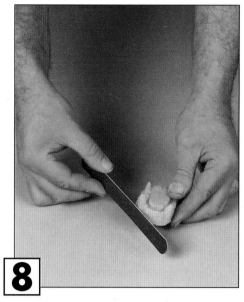

8

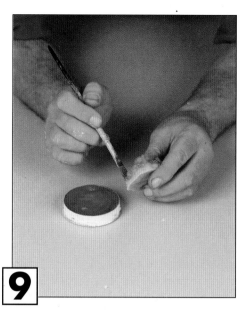

9

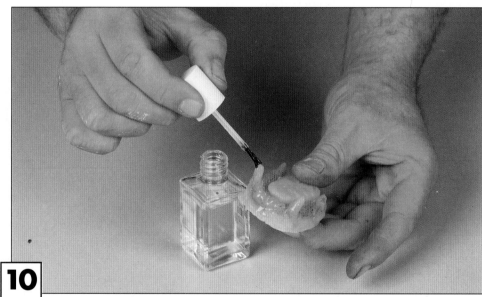

10

Eyes

Eyes can be bought from the taxidermy man ready-painted in hand-blown glass or as acrylic and glass shells which you can paint yourself (on the inside). [11] Glass shells have an indentation to match the shape of the pupil. Use oil paint or coloured nail varnish to paint first pupil, then iris, then outer part. [12] Marbles make excellent eyes. Paint them with oil paint then a final coat of five-minute epoxy glue for a wet and sparkling look.

Small balls of any material can be painted. Table Tennis balls are very light and avoid adding weight to the mask – but are easily dented.

11

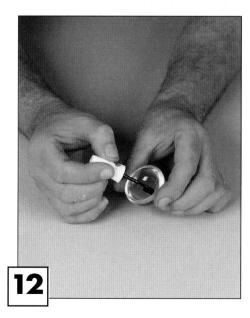

12

MAKING A HEAD PIECE

A head piece both provides a head-covering, either of hair or a headdress, and a way of securing the face mask to the head.

To make the simple head pieces used in this book seek out your local millinery supplier and obtain a couple of yards (metres) of anatomy net. This wonderful material is a net impregnated with glue which, when wet, becomes malleable and then dries fairly stiff. At the same time take a look at what else is for sale, you may find other interesting materials to use for mask-making.

While you are there buy some millinery wire to reinforce the edges of head pieces.

Preparations

First make your head block the same size as that of the wearer. You could

MATERIALS NEEDED

Head shape
Anatomy net
String
Millinery wire
1in (2.5 cm) ribbon for edging
Clingfilm (Saran Wrap)
Sticky tape
Rubber-based glue (Copydex)
Bowl of water
Scissors
Needle and thread
Hair, ribbons, headwear or other finish for the head according to design

rely on hat size or measure his or her head and then pad a smaller block up to match the size but an easy way is to use clingfilm (Saran Wrap) and sticky tape.

Wrap the clingfilm over your subject's head to form a cap over the forehead and down to the neck. Over this lay bands of sticky tape from front to back, side to side and around the whole to keep it from moving. With a marker pen drawn on the hairline as a guide to positioning.

Now take off the cap and set it on your head block, padding the inside with layers of paper until it makes a perfect fit. Of course, this only works for a larger head than your block. For a small head you just have to improvise a smaller block.

Set out your tools and materials and you are ready to begin.

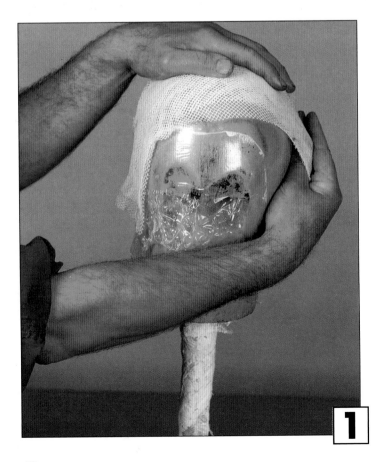

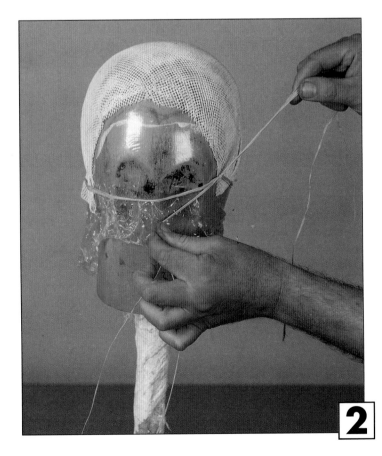

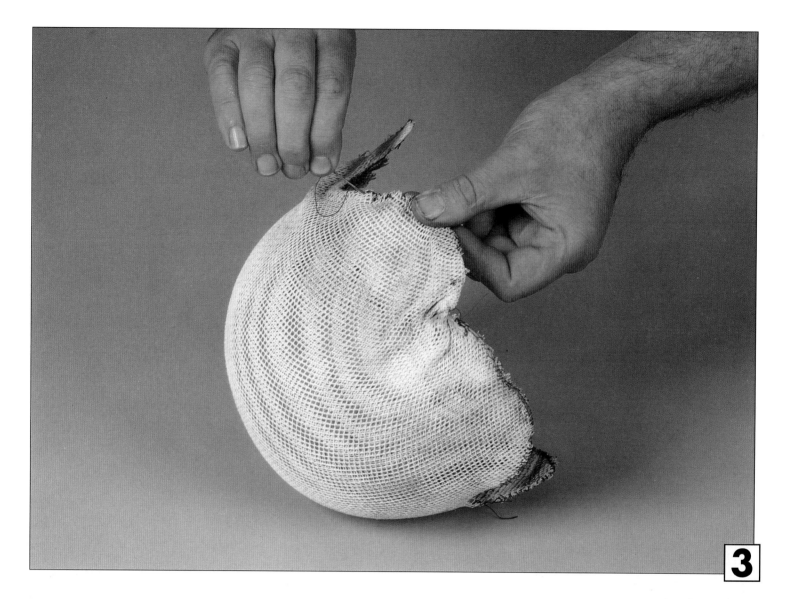

3

Constructing the head piece

Measure out enough anatomy net to cover the head block twice over (i.e. two layers). Lay one on top of the other and wet them in cold water. Milliners steam the net rather than dipping it in water and you may prefer to try that instead. However, either way it is important not to overdo it or you will wash out the glue. Squeeze out most of the water and place the double layers of net over the head shape. Allow an overlap of about 2 in (5 cm) all round beyond the final shape you require.[1]

Smooth it down to match the contours of the head and if necessary tie down the edges with a band of string. [2] Leave it to dry. You can accelerate the drying by placing the whole block in a warm (not hot) oven.

When the head piece is dry, ease it off the head shape and trim with scissors to the form you need – usually like a wig covering the whole head to the nape.

The head piece could be used in this raw state but it is better to reinforce the edge by stitching a wire around the edge [3] and then gluing or stitching ribbon over it for comfort.

Finishing the head piece

Cover the head block with clingfilm (if not already covered) to protect it. Then put the head piece back on the head block and apply whatever finish or decoration your design requires.

The easiest method is to stick hair, ribbons or pieces of cloth onto the net shape with a rubber- based adhesive such as Copydex. [4]

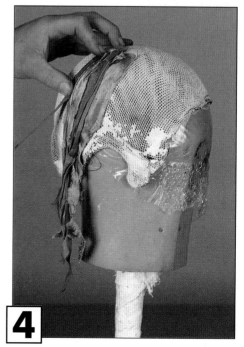

4

Circle the crown with hanging ribbons or hair and press them down over the top of the head, not just at the tip. If you wish you can layer them but this is not usually necessary. [5]

When you have finished adding pieces and the glue is dry, trim as needed. [6] Now ease the headpiece off the block. This will be made easier by cutting free the cling film underneath.

You do not have to use a hair-like treatment, whether locks, curls or syylized ribbons. Any covering or decoration suited to the mask's character can be applied.

Attaching the mask

Attaching the mask to the headpiece is best done on the wearer, though it

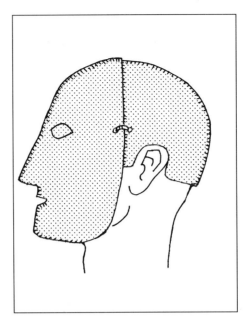

can be done on the head block if he or she is not available.

Put a piece of wire through the headpiece at a convenient point on both sides of the face to attach the mask then put the headpiece on. Place the mask in the ideal position on the face, adjusting to ensure that the wearer can see, breath and speak as necessary and mark on the mask points which match in with the position of the wires on the head piece. Now make holes in the mask and attach wire through them. Replace the mask and twist the wires together. While keeping the mask in place they will also allow it to pivot upwards so that headpiece and mask can be easily removed together and put on again as one piece. [7]

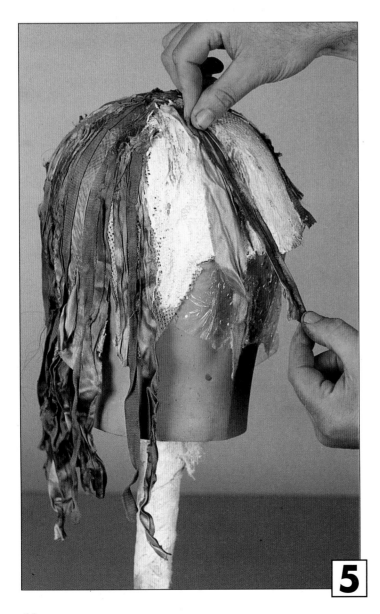

5

6

MAKING A CAST OF THE WHOLE HEAD

A whole head cast may be needed if you have to create a close fitting all-round mask rather than one of the face alone. A sculpt can be built up over it or a *papier mâché* or Celastic mask modelled directly on to it if you are making a mask for the upper part of the face which you want to carry over the head. (If you extend below the chin or below the dip at the back of the head you will not be able to remove it.)

A whole-head cast can also give an exact form for fitting a face mask to a fabric or anatomy net based rear part and finishing their dressing. You can use it as a basic head shape for any work on heads of similar size or masks which do not have to be a precise fit.

The method is identical to that used for casting a face but applied to the whole head. Of course it takes longer and requires considerably more trust and patience from the subject.

If a metal tube or rod is placed vertically in the centre of the neck before the plaster sets this can be inserted into a hole of comparable size drilled into a wooden stand, providing support for the cast when you want to work on it, or for display as a life cast.

In the example in the photograph not only the head but the neck and shoulders were cast. While not necessary for mask-making this forms a complete portrait study which, if the lower edge (of either a hollow or a solid cast) is allowed to form in a level horizontal plane, will produced a self-standing piece.

In making a complete head cast get someone to assist you. Not only will this considerably shorten the time during which your subject has to endure being covered in alginate and plaster bandages, it may also be the only way in which you can get it finished before the alginate goes off. It will help in making it more even resulting in a better mould.

MATERIALS NEEDED

(as for the face cast but in much greater quantities)

Cling film (Saran Wrap)
1 lb (453 gm) dental alginate (2 boxes)
Approx 20 4in x 6½ ft (10 cm x 2 m) plaster bandages (2 boxes)
11 lbs (5 kg) plaster of Paris
Petroleum jelly (Vaseline)
Cold water
2 plastic bowls for alginate
2 plastic buckets for plaster
1 plastic bowl for bandages
Plaster knife
Scissors
Brushes for applying plaster
Rasp
Metal rod (optional)
Swim cap (ideally a theatrical bald cap in which case you also need spirit gum)
and the person whose head is to be cast

Preparation

Get ready a clear working surface and your materials. Make the subject comfortable on a chair. Explain that the process will take 20 minutes or so. Protect the subject's hair with a bald cap, tucking the hair inside. Glue the cap on below the temples with spirit gum and use sticking plaster to secure it at the back of the neck, the forehead should hold without adhesive. Trim around the ears. Insert a little cotton wool in the ears, not sufficient to plug them but to make sure alginate does not go down the ear.

Protect the subjects clothing with a cloth or plastic garbage bag. If you are casting the shoulders these must be left bare.

Apply a smear of Vaseline over the eyebrows and any other facial or body hair to prevent it from becoming trapped in the alginate – not too much or the alginate won't stick.

Making the mould

Mix up 4-5 handfuls of alginate in one bowl, with another ready for your assistant to mix as soon as you start applying it. To slow its drying keep it as cold as possible – in hot weather add ice cubes to the water.

You begin to apply alginate to the face exactly as for the face cast and when he or she is ready, your assistant works on the back of the head. In both cases work downwards. If your alginate goes off before you finish your assistant's will still be useable. Work as fast as you can, you have a lot to cover, but make sure that you maintain a gentle, firm touch.

On the ears do a sweep around the back first and then gently apply into the ear.

Make sure that the alginate is about 1¾ in (2-2.5 cm) thick over the back of the head. If it is not thick enough it could tear as it is removed.

When the alginate is set, wet and apply plaster bandages as for the face cast.

Carry bandages over the face and front of the head forming a clean edge half way back and from left to right over the head. Double the bandage on this edge over and square it off more than usual. You need a clean smooth surface to which the back half will overlap but slide off when you want to seperate them.

When all the plaster bandages on the front are dry spread petroleum jelly generously over the edging strip. Then begin bandaging the back of the head, beginning with the top strip which should again be double, and brought forward over the edge which you have just covered in separator.

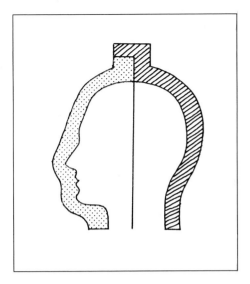

Work backwards to complete the bandage case and wait for it to dry. Reassure your subject that his or her ordeal is nearly over – remember how much weight their encased head is carrying!

As you wait for the bandages to dry make some clear marks across the join. This will help you to fit everything accurately back together again after removal.

Removing the mould

When the plaster bandages are hard – not before, you do not want to risk the case distorting – loosen the edge of the join between front and back halves and remove the back half plaster case in one piece and set it carefully aside.

Take a wooden modelling tool or a pair of scissors with the rounded blade towards the head and cut or slit open the alginate upwards from the centre back to just below the top of the head. If possible keep your fingers between the head and the implement.

Ask the subject to lean forward, holding the bandage case against the face, and pull faces to loosen the alginate from his or her features. With your assistant's help pull the flaps of alginate on either side of the slit you have made at the back upwards and forwards. Take care in releasing the ears. Do not hurry this stage, the alginate will rip if you are not careful. Keep your subject calm and still, even though they may want to struggle for release. Try to keep the alginate within the front plaster case.

You have no time to help your subject to clean up. You have to reconstruct the alginate and its outer casing.

Reconstructing the mould

With your assistant bring the back and front casing together, keeping the alginate in the front part and the back flaps out of the way. Make the guide lines you drew line up exactly.

Now apply wetted plaster bandage around the outside of the join back to front across the two halves and around the centre of the case.

You may find it helpful to upend the whole mould in a bucket to support it. Repair any rips in the alginate with express-drying `super-glue' (the best adhesive to bond alginate). Take care not to get any on your fingers or anywhere other than the edges you need to stick!

Making the cast

Mix up a bucket of plaster of Paris and, while your assistant slowly pours the mix into the mould, use your fingers to work the plaster into the ear spaces, the nose and other details. Either hollow out to reduce the weight of the cast or fill the mould with plaster. If you want to fix a head upon a stand push a metal tube (better because plaster can also flow up inside it) or a rod vertically into the neck before the plaster goes off and hold it there while it hardens.

When dry remove the plaster bandages, roll off the alginate (or rip it open if you have any difficulty,) and repair and tidy up any blemishes on the cast. If you have cast the shoulders mark the level which you wish to form the base and rasp away the plaster to form a smooth base on which your cast can rest.

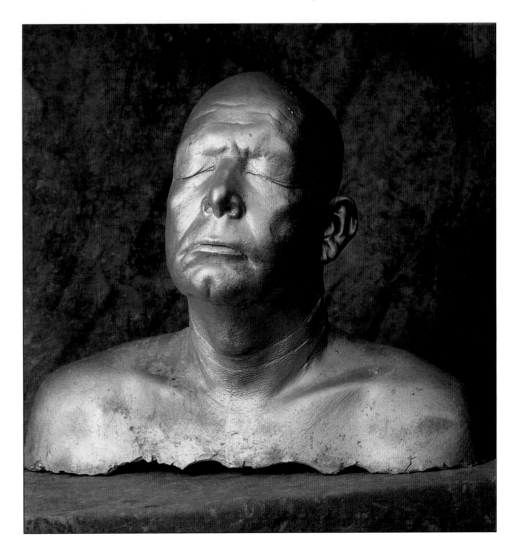

MAKING A
WHOLE-HEAD MASK

Sculpting a whole-head mask is much the same process as for making a face mask alone, but using considerably more clay! Build it up over a full head cast in the same way as you created a sculpt on the face mask. If you do not have a whole-head you could make a sculpt over a head block of approximately the right size.

The process of making the mould follows the same principles as for moulded face masks but, of course, you have to mould the rest of the head too. This mould is cast in two pieces which are then joined up to make a single mould.

MATERIALS NEEDED
Clay sculpt
Dental plaster (this is stronger than and preferable to plaster of Paris for the larger mould, though plaster of Paris can be used if dental plaster is not available)
Plaster bandage
Hessian (Plasterer's scrim) optional
Water
Mixing Bowl
Wood (baseboard and 2 x 2 in (5 x 5 cm) scrap timber will serve
Hammer
Clay
Petroleum jelly (Vaseline)
Paint brushes
Kidney tool or flexible ruler
Towel or cloth

Casting a whole-head mask
First you must sculpt the whole head in clay, as you want the final mask to be. [1]

Decide where the seam between the two halves is going to be. If it is a head with ears you have the choice of going around their edges or behind

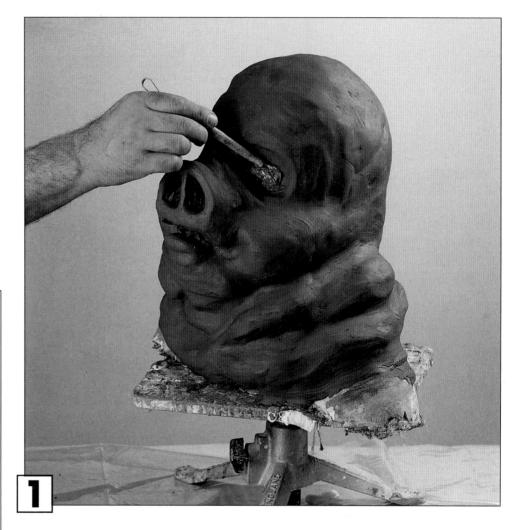

them. Along the edges is often easier because you do not then have to poke clay out of the ear when you remove the cast mould.

The two halves of the mould must butt precisely and to create this crisp edge a wood and clay wall, about 4in (12cm) thick is raised around the sculpt, technically known as the `ground up wall' because it is built from the working surface or base board upwards.

Building the ground up wall
On a level base board, place the sculpted head on its back, which will usually have less detail. Support it

with cloth or other padding to prevent damage and to keep it steady. Place pieces of scrap timber, at least 2 x 2 in (5 x 5cm) thick, around it to build up an encircling wall. [2] At the neck end, place a piece of wood across to keep the other edges rigid but otherwise leave it open. Keep the timber together with plaster bandages.[3]

Build the wall up nearly to the level where you plan the seam between the two halves of the mould. Now fill in the space between your sculpture and the wall with crumpled paper to reduce the amount of clay which you now spread over it to make

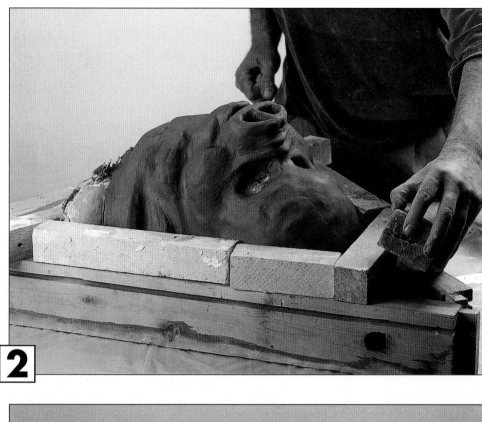

2

4

3

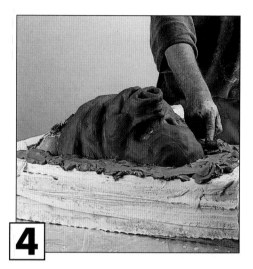

5

6

sculpture tool and gouge out a channel between the keys and about one inch (2.5 cm) out from the sculpture right around it. This will prevent liquid seeping out so easily from the complete mould when you cast your mask.

a level surface, bringing the clay over the top of your wooden surround. If you use a different colour clay for this it becomes easy to distinguish from the sculpt.

Create a very smooth surface for your top edge at the seam point and ensure that it joins up to your sculpture. A paint brush and a kidney tool or a flexible ruler will help you to make a good surface. Where this edge joins the sculpt make the join clean

and take off any imperfections. [5]

When you are satisfied with the edge gouge out four or five semi-spherical hollows around the perimeter, about 2 in (5cm) from the edge. [6] These will become `keys' which will precisely position the two halves of the mould when they are put together.

If you are going to make your mask by pouring a very fluid liquid, such as latex, take a rounded wire

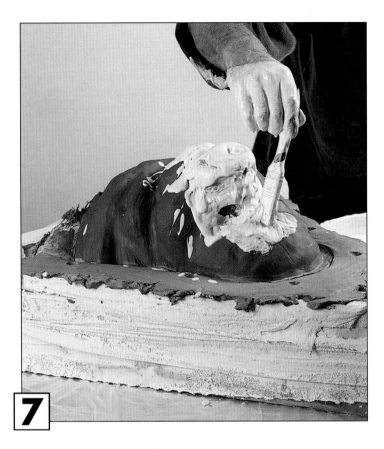

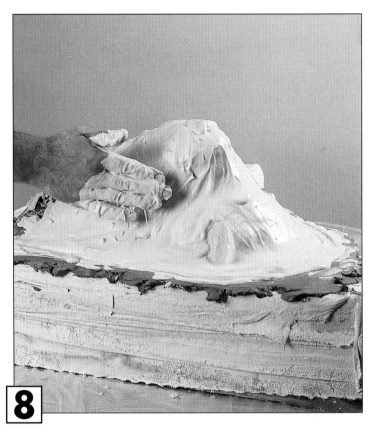

Making the first half of the mould

The mould is going to take quite a lot of plaster and you will need to make several mixes if it is not to `go off` before you use it. Mix the first batch and begin by gently brushing plaster over the details of the face and carefully into the keys. [7]

Layer by layer build up the plaster to a thickness of about one inch (2.5 cm) and draw up plaster that is flowing downwards. [8] Incorporate the open-weave hessian bandage known as plasterer's scrim as reinforcement if you wish, but do not add it until the first layers are well set or it may go into the surface of the mould and spoil its detail.[9] Mix more plaster as you need it.

As the plaster begins to set, but is still pliable, smooth over the outer surface with a wet sponge and shape up the edge to a tidy finish, but still keeping it thick for clamping later. [10] This will be much easier than trying when fully dry to remove jagged bits that could cut you or snag on things.

Now leave the plaster to complete its chemical process and harden.

Making the second half of the mould

Remove the `ground up wall`, and begin to carefully remove any clay which has adhered to your sculpture.

Turn sculpture and plaster over together – you will probably need help to do so – and rest with the plaster on your work surface. If there is any damage to its modelling or texture this is the time to make it good. Place some support around the plaster to keep the whole mass steady. Do not apply plaster to the second half yet. If you did, the plaster would stick to the half mould already made and you would not be able to get them apart. With a 1 in (2.5 cm) paintbrush apply a separator of petroleum jelly to the plaster edge of the half mould which you have just created.

To further facilitate the separation of the two halves of the mould lay two small wedges of clay about an $1/2$ in thick by 2 in wide (1.25 x 5 cm) on the edge of the half mould on opposite sides of the sculpture. These will give you a place to slip in a lever to make it easier to prize apart the two finished halves.

Now you are ready to apply the plaster to the second half in exactly the same way as you did the first. Be careful not to allow any plaster to run over onto the first half mould or you will have to smash the edge to separate them. While the plaster is going-off smooth it over with a sponge. When it is complete leave it until it is fully dry.

REMEMBER

Wash out plaster brushes as soon as you have finished working with them or they will become useless. Don't leave them while you wait for one half of the mould to dry – the plaster on the brush will dry long before the mould does!

Taking the mould apart

At this stage a second pair of hands will again be helpful. Make a clear workspace and place an old towel or cloth under the dry double mould to prevent it slipping about – it will probably be both heavy and awkward to handle. Use a lever in the wedges of clay to help prize the two halves

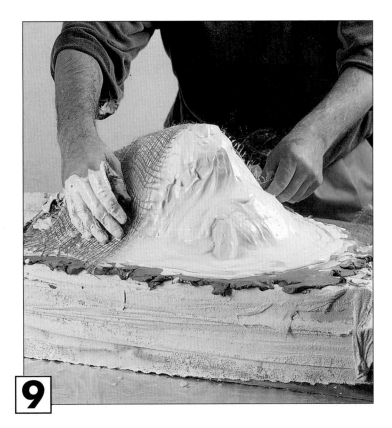

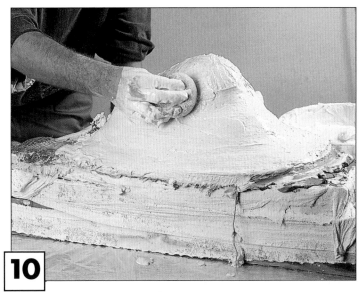

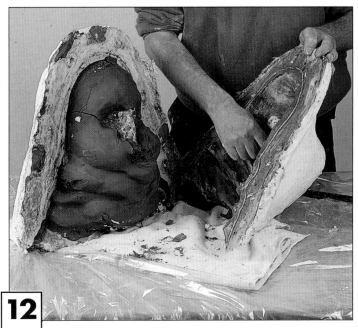

apart. [11] Do it gently, if half a mould shoots off your worktable it could smash. You may find it easier to do this on the floor.

If the separation proves difficult it may be because your sculpture has dried out too much. Pouring a little water into the base of it could help.

When you have the two halves apart use wooden tools to clean out any clay which has adhered to the plaster. [12] There is no urgency to do this, it can wait until you want to use the mould. If you are making a core piece as described below leave it until that has been cast.

Moulding in latex or with filler latex

MATERIALS NEEDED

Mould
Fluid latex or latex with filler
Paint brush
Scissors,
Craft knife
Small drill with fine bur disc
G-clamps or plaster bandages
Materials for colouring and
  finishing mask

Put the mould together and secure it with G-clamps or bind it with plaster bandage. Work along the seam with wet clay

Paint fluid latex into each half mould to ensure fine detail and then assemble the mould. Seal the seam with wet clay smoothing it over with a sponge. Paint latex across the seam and add additional layers. It may not be easy to see what you are doing with your arm inside the opening so make sure that the first coats are complete (except for the edges where you will apply clay) before you put it together.

If you are using latex with filler then pour in the latex and leave it for up to three hours before pouring it out again. In warm weather or hot climates a little less time is needed.

You will need to trim the seam and remove any imperfections with a file or an abrasive drill bit on a small drill – but use this carefully or you could hole your mask.

Colour and finish masks as already described for the face masks and head pieces.

However, for a full head mask the thin texture of these latex materials may not give you the solidity you require. An alternative which is often preferable is to use a foam material.

Making a foam mask

For casting a thicker foam mask a core piece must now be made. Used inside the mould this will leave a pocket between them into which the foam will be poured.

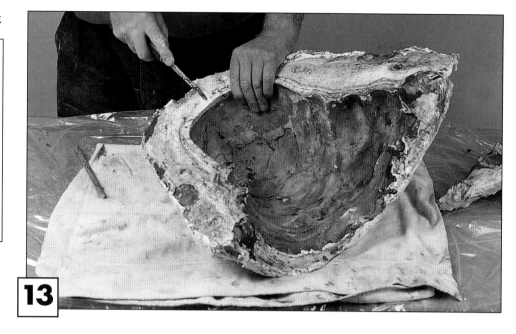

13

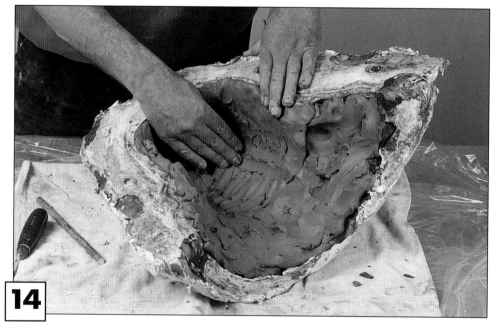

14

MATERIALS NEEDED

For the core:
Mould
Clay
Rolling pin (or large smooth bottle)
Plaster of Paris
Plaster bandage
Hessian (plasterer's scrim)
Petroleum jelly (Vaseline)
Water
Mixing bowl
6in (15cm) bolt or steel or
  aluminium rod

Lever
Rasp
For the mask:
Sponge
Water
G-clamp or old belt
Latex
Brush
Flexible polyurethane foam
  and activator
Scissors
Knife
Colouring and finishing materials

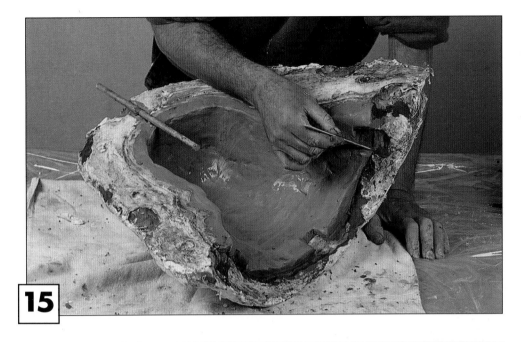

15

16

across any gap between the clay inside the two halves, smoothing it over with a wet sponge.

When the bandages are dry up-end the mould in a box or bucket padded with cloth or newspaper. Take care not to jar the bolt or rod. Apply petroleum jelly to the location squares you have cut and any plaster in the edges of the mould that has not been covered by clay.

Now mix up some plaster and pour it into the mould. [16] As it begins to harden work it up the sides of the clay lining until you have a thickness of about 3 in (7.5 cm), if necessary adding more plaster before the first application hardens. Strengthen with hessian if you feel it is needed. The plaster must come right up the sides to the opening of the mould and into the location squares. Tidy around the top with a damp sponge and leave it to harden.

When it is quite dry place the whole mould on the floor, supporting it with cloth to prevent damage, and strip off the plaster bandages. Use a lever in the pre-formed slots to help prize the halves of the mould apart and work evenly around the edges to separate it. Remove all the clay, washing it with a brush in a bucket of water if necessary, and tidy up the core – there are inevitably some rough edges to be filed off.

Next clean up the inside of the mould itself with a wet sponge. You must make sure no clay adheres. [17]

Making the core piece

Make a groove, just big enough to accept the thickness of a 6 in (5 cm) bolt or metal rod, at the top of one half of the mould. [13]

Take some clay and, on a smooth surface, roll it out with a rolling pin (or a bottle will do) to a sheet about two inches thick. Lay this into one section of the mould like pastry into a pie-dish and press it gently into the mould, especially over the face. [14] Trim off the edge of the clay level with the edge of the mould. Do the same for the other half of the mould.

Around the base (neck end) of the mould cut out squares from the clay to act as location markers. [15]

Fit the two halves of the mould together with the bolt or rod sticking through it with at least 2 1/2 in (7cm) projecting into the mould beyond the clay.

Bind the two sections of the mould together with an old belt or plaster bandage, then apply plaster bandages along the seam.

Take some wet clay and seal

17

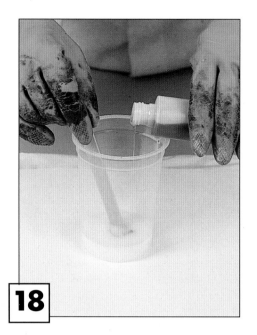

18

For masks with very fine detail paint a first coat of latex into the detail before you assemble the mould. Remember to seal the seam between halves with clay before pouring in more latex to coat it all over.

Casting the foam mask

Reassemble the mould with G-clamps and a belt or plaster bandages.

Support the mould and lower in the core, fitting the bolt into its hole and matching the location squares to the sockets for them in the rim of the mould.

19

Latex is better than most flexible polyfoams at holding detail so next pour latex into the mould, filling it to the top, do this slowly so that the air is expelled as it enters. After a few minutes pour it out again and back into its container. Leave the latex to dry, preferably overnight. It must be completely dry before you pour in the polyfoam. When the latex is dry, mix up the polyfoam or other material you have chosen according to the maker's instructions. [18]

Pour the polyfoam into the mould [19] where it will foam up. You will not be able to see the process but [20] shows it happening in a clear container.

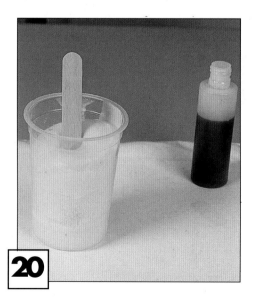

20

WARNING
If the latex is not completely dry when you pour polyfoam onto it the foam will collapse into a sticky mess.

DANGER
Polyfoam gives off toxic fumes. When working with it, it is ESSENTIAL to keep the room WELL VENTILATED. ALWAYS wear rubber gloves when using polyfoam.

The polyfoam should be left for half an hour. In warm months the foam may activate more rapidly than in winter. Then you can take the mould apart.

Once the outer mould has been removed the mask can be rolled off the centre core. There may be large amounts of superfluous material to trim off at the seam between the two halves of the mould. Do this with scissors and a heated knife. Take care not too cut deeply, or you may find you have cut through the walls between the foam and made a hole. Heat a knife to melt rather than cut off small imperfections. It may help to seal over any small holes or imperfections too.

DANGER
Heat from the knife produces toxic fumes. Make sure the windows are open.

If any tiny holes remain squeeze in a little rubber adhesive (Copydex), mixing in a very small amount of cellulose filler for slightly larger holes. Set the mask aside to dry before colouring and finishing. Sometimes, as in the pig mask shown in the illustrations to this chapter, some parts are difficult to include in the sculpt. Here it was the ears which hang away from the head. They were cut from latex painted in several layers on a flat surface to the thickness required and then glued to the head.[21]

21

Masks made from two-part moulds:

A squirrel head-mask, made in a double mould. A mask which sits on top of the head, rather than over the face, is often the best solution for some animals. It also avoids all the problems of being able to see, breathe and speak without impediment.

Several of these masks were required, to be worn by different performers. Instead of creating each individually, all the masks were made from the same mould in the form of a thick latex skin. Inside each was fitted a Celastic former, individually fitted to the wearer and fixed with hot glue. These liners ensured that each mask was a perfect fit for the performer who wore it.

To keep costs down the eyes were included into the sculpt and painted in the latex. Because the hair was required to be short all over it had to be hand laid, not in weft. Six colours were mixed to give interest. The whiskers were bristles from a broom, glued into position

Below

Bird masks, also designed to sit on the top of the head. The plumage is made up of both pads of feathers and strings of feathers regularly applied from the neck upwards to overlap each other following the natural lay. The whole masks were made in a double mould using latex with a filler, the beaks being smoothed down with a sponge before they were completely dry and then sprayed with an acrylic varnish to make them look hard and glossy.

Above

A carnival mask, about three feet (90 cm) across. This was made in Celastic using a two-part mould and was designed to rest on the shoulders. It does not fit closely to the face so there was no need to use a head cast in sculpting it. Bringing the ears onto the front face made casting easier and a similar design could be made as a frontal mask.

Right

A latex mask made for a dancer. A pair of masks were needed for two dancers but to keep cost down the same mould was used for both. The latex was sufficiently flexible for both to fit reasonably well.

The nostrils were cut to allow them to breathe but they were not required to speak or sing so the mouth was left closed. However, to increase ventilation, small pin holes were made with a hot needle over the surface of the mask. These would not be visible to an audience but made the mask more comfortable for an active performer.

A mask of the Egyptian god Anubis, again designed to be worn on the top of the head. The shape and position of the ears made a join in the case from left to right impractical so the seam was planned from front to back along the ridge of the muzzle. The residual seam when the mask was moulded in latex with a filler was neatly abraded away with an acrylic bur used on a modelling drill. However, gold paint tends to show up any irregularities and so the pigment was mixed with PVA. This would have been a good subject on which to apply a gilding of an inexpensive form of gold leaf.

A goat's head mask, made in a two-part mould with the join down the nose. This was intended to make it easier to remove the horns from the mould but results were not to the maker's satisfaction and instead the horns were cast separately in acrylic (as described on pages 60-61 for teeth) and then attached to the mask. The glass eyes were set into the sculpt, then removed before casting the mould, creating an exact cavity into which to place them in the finished mask. On the muzzle, mixed yak hair was applied with spirit gum but, over the rest of the face, weft hair was used, which can be fixed much more quickly. The wearer can see out through the mouth aperture.

This mask was made in latex with a filler, further reinforced with hessian. This proved very heavy. Polyfoam would have produced a much lighter mask but would have required the making of a core.

STOCKISTS AND SUPPLIERS

Most of the materials that you need for mask-making can be obtained from theatrical suppliers, art and craft and sewing shops. Dental suppliers will have aginate and acrylic monomers. For local sources try your Yellow Pages under headings such as these under latex, rubber and ceramic supplies.

If you cannot find sources locally a number of stockists will supply by mail order. Some are listed below.

UNITED STATES

CLAY

Leisure Crafts Co,
30 E 19 St, New York 1003

PLASTER

Earth Materials
588 Myrtle Ave, Brooklyn, NY

US Gypsum Co
101 S Walker Drive Chigago, IL 60606

SCULPTURE TOOLS

Sax Arts and Crafts
PO Box 2002 Milwaukee, WI 53201

Sculpture House
38 E 30 St, New York, NY 10016

LATEX

Alcone Co Inc
5-49 Ave, Long Island City, NY 11101

R &D Latex Corp
5901 Telegraph Rd, Commerce CA 90040

CELASTIC

Alcone Co Inc
5-49 Ave, Long Island City, NY 11101

Body Parts
PO Box 503 Newton Center MA 02159

PLASTER BANDAGES

Body Parts
PO Box 503 Newton Center MA 02159

Titius Health Care
160 Garfield, Alhambra CA 91801

POLYURETHANE FOAMS

BJB Enterprises
6350 Industry Way, Westminster CA 92683

Burman Polysoft
20930 Almazan Rd, Woodland Hills CA 91650

DENTAL SUPPLIERS

Davis Dental Co
13056 Saticoy St, N Hollywood, Ca 91605

Henry Schein Inc
5 Harbour Park Drive, Port Washington, NY 11050

Lang Dental Mfg Co Inc.
2300 W Wabansia, Chicago IL 60647

HAIR AND WIGS

California Theatrical Supplies
123 9th St, San Francisco CA 94103

Cinema Secrets Inc,
2909 W Olive St, Burbank CA 91505

ACETONE

Tri-Eee Science
622 W Colorado, Glendale CA 91204

TAXIDERMY SUPPLIES

Van Dyke's Taxidermy Supplies
Woonsocket SD 57385

UNITED KINGDOM

CLAY

A Tiranti
70 High Street, Reading, Berkshire

The Fulham Pottery
8-10 Ingate Place, London SW8

PLASTER

A. Tiranti
70 High Street, Reading, Berkshire

Dawson Co,
Mendip Wharf, York Rd,
Battersea, London SW11

The Fulham Pottery
8-10 Ingate Place, London SW8

LATEX

A Tiranti
70 High Street, Reading, Berkshire

G.M. Foam Kits
47 Copers Cope Rd, Beckenham, Kent BR3 1NJ

D.B. Shipping
St Margarets's House
18-20 Southwark St, London SE1 1TJ

CELASTIC

A Tiranti
70 High Street, Reading, Berkshire

G.M. Foam Kits
47 Copers Cope Rd, Beckenham, Kent BR3 1NJ

PLASTER BANDAGES

The Fulham Pottery
8-10 Ingate Place, London SW8

Charles Fox
22 Tavistock St, London WC2

POLYURETHANE FOAMS

Bonda Voss
158-160 Ravenstock Rd, Beckenham, Kent

Foam Systems UK
42 Trentham Rd, Hartshill, Nuneaton, Warwicks CV10 0SN

DENTAL ALGINATE

Cottell & Co
15-17 Charlotte St, London W1P 2AA
(also in Edinburgh, Manchester and Swansea)

HAIR AND WIGS

A.H. Isles Ltd
146 Lower Rd, London SE16 2UG

Hairraisers
1-4 Fingest House, Lilestone St, London NW8

ACETONE

A Tiranti
70 High Street, Reading, Berkshire

TAXIDERMY

Snowdonia Taxidermy Studios
Llanrwst, Gwynedd, Wales LL26 0HU

AUSTRALIA

CLAY

Russell Cowan Pty Ltd.
128 Pacific Highway, Waitara, NSW 2077

PLASTER

Investo Manufacturing Co
33 Grand Ave, Camellia, NSW 2142

Film Make-up Technology
43-47 Trafalgar St, Annandale, NSW 2036

LATEX

Film Make-up Technology
43-47 Trafalgar St, Annandale, NSW 2036

Daystar Pty Ltd.
396 Princes Highway, Rockdale, NSW 2216

PLASTER BANDAGES

Film Make-up Technology
43-47 Trafalgar St, Annandale, NSW 2036

DENTAL ALGINATE

Film Make-up Technology
43-47 Trafalgar St, Annandale, NSW 2036

Dental House, Dental Supply
5th Floor, 332 Pitt St, Sydney NSW 2000